Anonymous

Outline of the History of the English Language and Literature

Anonymous

Outline of the History of the English Language and Literature

ISBN/EAN: 9783337084608

Printed in Europe, USA, Canada, Australia, Japan

Cover: Foto ©ninafisch / pixelio.de

More available books at **www.hansebooks.com**

OUTLINE OF THE HISTORY

OF

THE ENGLISH LANGUAGE

AND

LITERATURE

W. & R. CHAMBERS
LONDON AND EDINBURGH
1882

Edinburgh :
Printed by W. & R. Chambers.

PREFACE.

THE object of this book, as indicated in the title, is to give an outline of the History of the English Language and Literature.

It aims, however, at being something more than a mere statement of facts. It is intended to excite an interest in English philology, and in the leading authors that from the time of Cædmon have used the English tongue.

It is therefore to be regarded as an introduction to English philology and literature ; and is adapted for use in the advanced classes of elementary schools, in secondary schools, and for pupil teachers, as well as for private students.

CONTENTS.

LANGUAGE.

LITERATURE.

THE ENGLISH LANGUAGE.

CHAPTER I.
History of its Vocabulary.

1. **WHAT A LANGUAGE IS.**—A language is a number of different sounds which are made by the tongue and the other organs of speech. But a spoken language is, or may be, written or printed upon paper by the aid of a number of signs or symbols—which are generally printed in black ink upon white paper.—The parts of a spoken language are called sounds; the smallest parts of a written or printed language are called letters.—A language is also called a *tongue* or a *speech*.—A language, like a living being, does not remain always the same. It *grows*. As it grows, it alters in appearance; small and great changes take place in it; and the story of these changes is called the *History of the Language.*

2. **THE ENGLISH LANGUAGE** is the name given to the language which is spoken in Great Britain and Ireland, in the United States, in Canada, in Australia and New Zealand, in South Africa, and in many other parts of the world where Englishmen, Scotchmen, and Irishmen are found. In the middle of the fifth century it was spoken by a few thousand

men who came over to Britain from the north-west of Europe, and by many thousands of men and women who dwelt on the banks of the lower parts of the great German rivers—the Rhine, the Elbe, and the Weser. It is now spoken by more than 100 millions of people. But the English spoken in the fifth century was a very different language from the English that is spoken now. It was different, yet still the same. It was different in appearance, as a child of one year old is different in looks from a man of forty; but both the English of to-day and the English of the fifth century are the same—because the one has grown out of the other, just as the tall strong man of forty has grown out of the child of one year old.

3. FAMILY.—To what family of languages does our English speech belong? It belongs to the **Indo-European family** of languages. This family is so called, because the languages which belong to it are spoken both in India and in Europe. Many thousand years ago, the people from whom we are descended lived on the high table-lands in the heart of Asia. Bands of them kept travelling always farther and farther west; and it is from their language that most of the tongues spoken in Europe are derived. These bands left their friends and relations and country, just as young men and women nowadays leave the homes of their parents to go and settle in distant countries. The Indo-European is also called the Aryan family of languages. Altogether, it embraces seven great languages—(1) The Indian or Sanskrit; (2) Persic; (3) Greek; (4) Latin; (5) Keltic; (6) Teutonic; and (7) Slavonic, which includes Russian, Polish, &c.

4. TEUTONS.—The English language was introduced into this country by bands of warlike colonists from North-western Germany, who drove the old inhabitants to the mountainous regions in the west of the island. Those colonists were variously called Angles, Saxons, and Jutes; but they all belonged to the Teutonic race, and their speech was a branch of the Teutonic group of languages. The Teutonic group of languages contains three main sections, from which all the others spring. These three main sections

are: **High-German, Low-German,** and **Scandinavian.** High-German is the name given to the kind of German which is spoken on the higher lands or table-lands of South Germany —those table-lands which slope from the Central Plain of Europe up to the Alps; and its northern boundary is the pretty river *Main*, which falls into the Rhine. Low-German is the name given to the kind of German spoken in the lowlands of Germany; and the southern boundary of this kind of speech is the river Main—its northern boundary being the Baltic and the North Sea. Scandinavian is the wide general name given to those kinds of Teutonic speech which are found in Denmark, Norway, Sweden, and Iceland. These divisions may be placed in a table in the following manner:

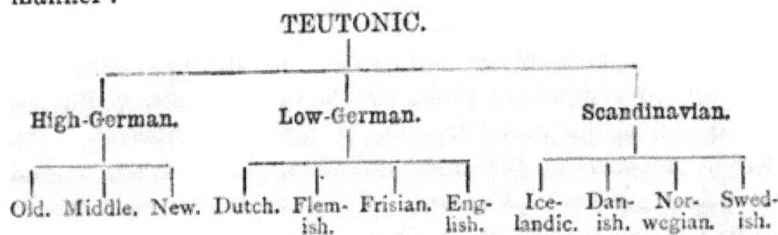

TEUTONIC.

High-German.			Low-German.			Scandinavian.			
Old.	Middle.	New.	Dutch.	Flem-ish.	Frisian.	Eng-lish.	Ice-landic.	Dan-ish.	Nor-wegian.	Swed-ish.

5. **HIGH-GERMAN.**—High-German is spoken in the southern parts of Germany—such as Bavaria, Swabia, and other hilly regions; and also in the north and east of Switzerland. —It is this form of the language that has become the book-speech or literary language of the Germans; and its technical name is **New High-German.**

6. **LOW-GERMAN.**—The languages which belong to this division are spoken in the plains of Germany, especially along the lower courses of the rivers, in Holland, in part of Belgium, in England, Scotland, and Ireland, and the British Colonies, and in the United States of North America. The Low-German spoken in Holland is called *Dutch;* the Low-German spoken in Belgium is called *Flemish;* the Low-German spoken in Friesland—a wealthy province of Holland—is called *Frisian;* and the Low-German spoken in England is called *English.* (But, as we shall soon see, English contains many thousands of words in addition

to those which are purely Low-German.) The language on the continent which is most like English is the Frisian language. There is indeed a well-known couplet, every word in which is said to be both Frisian and English. It runs thus:

> Good butter and good cheese
> Is good English and good Fries.

The following are the chief subdivisions of

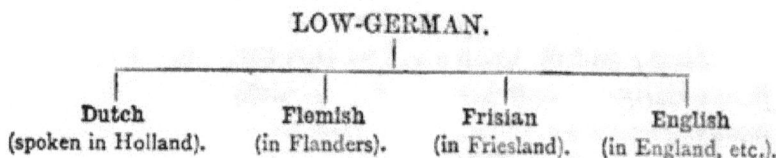

LOW-GERMAN.

Dutch	Flemish	Frisian	English
(spoken in Holland).	(in Flanders).	(in Friesland).	(in England, etc.).

7. **SCANDINAVIAN.**—Scandinavian is the general name given to the different kinds of Teutonic speech which are employed in Denmark, Norway, Sweden, and Iceland. The oldest and purest kind of Scandinavian speech is that spoken in the far-off country in the middle of the North Atlantic, called Iceland; and it is the purest, because for many centuries there has been very little communication with that country. Indeed, the Icelandic of the 12th century differs very little from the Icelandic of to-day. But the English of the twelfth century differs so much from the English of the nineteenth century, that we should at first sight hardly know them for the same speech.—One peculiar mark of a Scandinavian speech is the preference for hard consonants—the preference, for example, of a *k* over a *ch* or *sh*. Thus the Danes say *Dansk* for *Danish;* and it is Danish influence that has given to Scotchmen and to the north of England the form *kirk* instead of *church.*

8. **THE THREE CHIEF TEUTONIC LANGUAGES.**—The three most important languages belonging to the great Teutonic stock are **English, Dutch, and German.** If we look at the words used in these languages, we shall at once see that they are sister-languages. If we look at the way in which their words are changed—or at their inflections—we shall also see

that they are very closely related. Thus the commonest words appear in these three languages in the following shape :

English...........Three.	Mother.	Brother.	Have (inf.).
Dutch.............Drie.	Moeder.	Broeder.	Hebben.
German...........Drei.	Mutter.*	Bruder.†	Haben.

Again, the inflections of these three languages are very similar —are in fact, different shapes of the same changes. Thus the possessive case of nouns in all three languages ends in **s** or **es**‡ or **'s**. The second person singular of verbs in all three ends in *st ;* and the ending of the past participle in all three is generally *en*. We know, then, both from history and from a comparison of the actual facts in the present state of the languages, that all three are sister-tongues.

9. **WHERE THE ENGLISH CAME FROM.**—Those Teutons who brought over the English tongue to this island, came from the north-west of Europe—most of them from that part of the German coast which lies between the river Elbe and the river Weser. The kind of Low-German spoken by them is much the same as that still spoken in the lowlands of Hanover, Holstein, and Schleswig. There is in Holstein— upon the west coast—a small district which is called Angeln— that is, *England*—to this day. The Teutons who came over to Britain belonged to three tribes. They were Jutes and Angles and **Saxons**. The Jutes came from Jutland.§ The Angles came from Schleswig and Holstein. The Saxons came from Hanover and the land to the west of it. The Jutes settled in Kent and the Isle of Wight. The Saxons settled in Essex (or East Sex), Wessex || (or West Sex), Sussex (or South Sex), and Middlesex ; and the ending *sex* is an indication of the fact. The Angles settled chiefly in the north and east. One of the kingdoms founded by them was called East Anglia ; and the northern and southern settlers

---

* Pronounced *Mootter*.   † Pronounced *Brooder*.
‡ Thus we have *Wedneṣday* = the **day** of Woden or Odin.
§ *Jutland* means the *land of the Jutes; not* the *land that juts out.*
|| The division called **Wessex** included *Hampshire, Wiltshire, Berkshire, Somersetshire, Dorsetshire, Gloucestershire,* and *Devonshire.*

in it gave their names to the two counties of Norfolk and Suffolk, which are only later forms of the words *North folk* and *South folk*. These three tribes all spoke different dialects of the same speech. The early predominance of the Angles, especially as the Angles in Northumbria were the first to have a literature, gave to the language the name of *English*, though the Keltic people still call it *Saxon* or *Sassenach*. The country also in time acquired, from the same cause, the name of *Engla-land*, or the *land of the English*. The first landing of Teutons took place in the year 449; and for about a hundred years afterwards, bands of strong young warriors and colonists continued to arrive at short intervals.

10. **THE PERIODS OF ENGLISH.**—The language brought over to Britain by these three tribes has grown very much since the fifth century. It has been growing for fourteen hundred years. It has therefore altered very much in every way; its appearance has changed; and we have to learn the English of the fifth, or the eighth, or the eleventh century, almost as if it were a foreign language. There are four chief periods in the history of the English language. These are :

    I. Old English, commonly called Anglo-Saxon....450–1100
    II. Early English................................1100–1250
    III. Middle English............................. 1250–1485
    IV. Modern English..............................1485–1882

But it must not be forgotten that there is no hard and fast line between one period and another. A living language, like a living body, is always changing. It takes on new additions of new matter; it loses the old. With these new additions, its form also changes. We are rarely sensible of these changes; but they are going on all the time for all that.

11. **THE OLDEST ENGLISH OR ANGLO-SAXON, 450–1100.**— This form of the English language contained a very large number of inflections. The definite article was inflected for gender, number, and case; nouns and adjectives were highly inflected; and the verb had a very much larger number of inflections than it has now. The words of the English

vocabulary during this period were almost entirely English ; a few Latin and Greek words—brought in chiefly by the church—and a few Keltic words, had found their way into the English vocabulary. The rhyme used in poetry was not end-rhyme, as at the present date, but head-rhyme or alliteration—as we find it in the well-known line from Pope :

Apt alliteration's artful aid.

To this period belong the writings of the poet Cædmon and of King Alfred.

12. EARLY ENGLISH, 1100-1250.—The Normans had seized all power in the state and in the church, and had held it since the year 1066. During the early part of this period, English was not written, had ceased to be employed in books ; and French words began to creep in even among the spoken words of the English people. The inflections of words began to drop off, or to be carelessly used, and then to be mixed up and confused with each other. One of the chief writers of this period is a priest called Layamon, who wrote a poem called the *Brut* (*Brutus*), which gave some account of the beginnings of the English people, who were believed to be descended from Brutus, the fabled son of Æneas of Troy.

13. MIDDLE ENGLISH, 1250-1485.—Nouns and adjectives during this period lost almost all their inflections. The inflections of verbs were very much altered and greatly simplified.—In the year 1349, boys in school were allowed to cease translating their Latin into French, and began to translate it into English. In the year 1362 Edward III. passed an act of parliament ordering the use of English in the pleadings of cases in all courts of law, instead of Norman-French, which had hitherto been employed. To the first half of this period belong such works as the *Metrical Chronicle* and the *Lives of the Saints,* supposed to have been written and translated by Robert of Gloucester ; to the second half belong the works of the great poet Chaucer, of William Langland, and of the reformer Wicliffe.

14. MODERN ENGLISH, 1485-1882.—The year 1485 marks

the accession of the House of Tudor to the throne, in the person of Henry VII. By this time almost all inflections had disappeared from our language. Many hundreds of French words had come into the language. From the time of the Revival of Letters*—which may be said to have begun in the sixteenth century—several thousands of Latin words were poured into the English vocabulary. The period which lies between 1485 and 1603—the year in which James I. came to the throne—is sometimes called the period of **Tudor English.** Its greatest verse-writer is Shakspeare ; its greatest prose-writer is Hooker, who wrote *The Laws of Ecclesiastical Polity.*

15. ENGLISH WORDS IN THE ENGLISH LANGUAGE.—The English language has for centuries been importing words from many foreign tongues into its own vocabulary ; and it has given a hearty welcome to all kinds of strangers. So much is this the case, and so far has this habit of taking in strangers gone, that we can now quite accurately say : *Most of the words in our English language are not English.* There are more Latin words in our tongue than there are English. But this statement is true only of our words as we find them *in the dictionary.* The words which we use every day—the language *of the mouth*—is almost entirely English. The *fixed vocabulary*—the vocabulary printed in the dictionary—is more Latin than English ; the *moving vocabulary*—the words which are daily spoken—is English. Thus, if we take a passage in our translation of the Four Gospels, we shall find from 90 to 96 per cent. of the words used are English —and pure English. In the *Prologue* which Chaucer wrote to his famous set of poems called *The Canterbury Tales,* 88 per cent. of the words are English ; while, in Mrs Browning's *Cry of the Children,* the English words rise to the large proportion of 92 per cent.

The following is a list of a few more percentages of

---

* The Revival of Letters, or the Renascence (or *Renaissance*), is the name given to the new enthusiasm which seized Italians, Germans, Frenchmen, and Englishmen, in the fifteenth and sixteenth centuries, to read the great treasures of literature that may be found in Greek and Latin books.

purely English words in the writings of well-known authors :

Spenser (*Faerie Queene*, ii. 7)..........................86 per cent.
Shakspeare (*Henry IV., Part I.*, Act ii).............91 „
Milton (*Paradise Lost*, Book VI.)....................80 „
Swift (*John Bull*)...85 „
Johnson (Preface to *Dictionary*)......................72 „
Gibbon (*Decline and Fall of the Roman Empire*,
I., cap. vii.)..70 „
Macaulay (*Essay on Lord Bacon*)....................75 „
Tennyson (*In Memoriam*, first twenty poems)......89 „

16. CHANGES IN ENGLISH.—Let us take a passage from the Saxon translation of the Old Testament—and it is the oldest English version we have—and notice what differences there are between this English and the English of the present day. This translation was made by Abbot Ælfric, who lived and wrote late in the tenth century. He translated into English the five books of Moses—commonly called the Pentateuch— Joshua, Judges, and part of the book of Job. Let us see how he writes (Genesis, ix. 1):

God bleĩsode	God blessed
Noe and his suna	Noah and his sons
and cväd hem tô :	and quoth to them :
Veahxað	Wax (ye)
and beoð gemenigfilde	and be manifolded
and áfyllað	and fill
þâ eorðan !	the earth !

Now every word in the above verse is modern English ; but every word has been changed—with the exception of *God, his,* and *and*. All the other words have changed enormously in the course of the eight centuries since the verse was written. The words have changed ; and the grammar has changed. The word *bletsian* has become *bless*. The grammar of the verbs has changed enormously. For example, the imperative ending *ath* in *Veahxath* and *áfyllath* has quite fallen away. It existed, in the form of *eth*, down to the time of Chaucer, who writes *Standeth up !* in addressing several persons.—Next, we ought to notice that *all* the words are pure English. The modern

version which we still use, and which was published in 1611,
has been obliged to use Latin and French words. It says—
and the words in italics are all foreign words : 'Be *fruitful*, and
multiply and *replenish* the earth'! That is, it employs three
Latin words in the most important parts of the sentence.

17. **LOSS AND GAIN.**—But, while the English language has,
in the course of centuries, lost almost all its inflections, it has
been all that time gaining new words, and at the same time
gaining new powers of expression. In fact, the history of
our language is a history of both loss and gain. It has lost
inflections and gained new *words*. An inflected language is
generally called a **Synthetic Language**, because it expresses
changes of relations by the *adding-on (synthesis)* of something
to the end of the word. A language which expresses
relations by little words like prepositions is called an
analytic language. We may therefore say that :

> English was in its earlier forms a synthetic language ; but
> it is now an analytic language.

So much for the form or grammar of it. But, on the other
hand, if we look at the matter or words or vocabulary of it,
we shall find that :

> English was originally a pure or unmixed language ; but is
> now an extremely composite one.

18. **THE FOREIGN ELEMENTS IN ENGLISH.**—These have
come into our language chiefly because the English people
have come so much into contact with other peoples and
tribes and nations. They came over to this island in the
fifth century, and found Kelts here ; and from them they
took some Keltic words. About the end of the eighth
century, the Danes came to them ; and a number of Danish
words entered the language. Then another set of Danes or
Scandinavians—called Normans—came to them, conquered
them, and gave them many hundred Norman-French words.
Then, with the Revival of Letters, many scholars came over
here, taught the English people to read Greek and Latin
books ; and these books gave the language several thousand
words. Then the English people have always been the

greatest travellers in the world. They have gone to China and brought home Chinese words (as well as things) ; they have long held India, which has given us Hindu words ; they have imported names and terms from North and from South and Central America ; they have borrowed from Spaniards and Italians ; they have taken words, nearer home, from the Dutch and from the Germans ; they have gone to the farthest east and to the farthest west, and there is hardly a language on the face of the globe from which they have not imported some words that live and make themselves useful in our language.

19. **WELSH.**—When the English settled in this island, they found a people who were called Britons, and who spoke a language called **British** or **Kymric**. It is a language very different from English; and at first the English warriors and the British people did not understand one single word of what each other said. The Old English word for *foreigners* was *Wealhas*— or, as we call it now, *Welsh;* and the English fighting men who came over called the British people, not by the name which they themselves used, but simply the *foreigners*—the *Welsh*. In the same way, a German to this day calls an Italian or a Frenchman a *Welshman;* and he calls France or Italy *Welsh-land*. The language spoken by the Welsh belongs to the **Keltic group** of languages. This group contains also **Erse,** which is spoken in the west of Ireland ; **Manx**, which is spoken in the Isle of Man ; **Gaelic**, which is spoken in the Highlands of Scotland ; and **Breton,** which is spoken in Brittany—a mountainous and rugged peninsula in the north-west of France. It at one time embraced also **Cornish**—the language spoken in Cornwall, which was also called *West Wales*. But that language died out in 1778 ; and it is not now spoken by any one. The following is a table of the Keltic group :

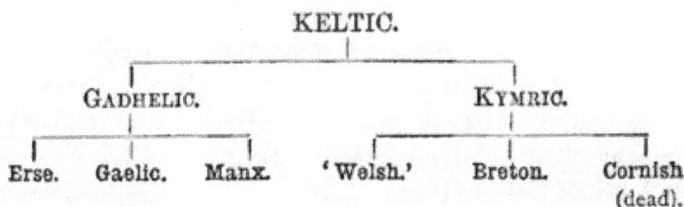

KELTIC.

GADHELIC.			KYMRIC.		
Erse.	Gaelic.	Manx.	'Welsh.'	Breton.	Cornish (dead).

20. **THE KELTIC ELEMENT.**—The words given to the English language by the Kelts are of two kinds :

(i) Names of mountains, rivers, lakes, and other natural features;

(ii) Names of common things, which the English picked up in their daily intercourse with the British or Welsh.

(i) The Keltic name for a mountain is *Pen*—a word which we find in *Pennine* and *Apennine*. The Gaelic or Scotch Keltic form of the word is *Ben*. Thus we have *Ben More*—which means the *Big Mountain—Ben Nevis*, and many others. The commonest Keltic word for a river is *Avon*. There are fourteen Avons in Great Britain. *Esk* is another common Keltic name for a river; and there are eight *Esks* in Scotland alone. In England the name takes the form of *Ex* or *Exe* (the consonants having changed places, *Ex* = *Eks*). The name appears as *Ex* in *Exeter* (the old form was *Exanceaster*)—that is, *the camp on the Ex ;* as *Ax* in *Axminster ;* as *Ox* in *Oxford ;* as *Ux* in *Uxbridge ;* as *Usk,* in Wales ; and even as *Ouse,* in Yorkshire and other counties.—*Aber* is a Keltic word which means *the mouth of a river ;* and we find it in *Aberdeen* (the town at the mouth of the Dee); *Arbroath,* which is = *Aber-brothock ; Aberystwith ; Berwick*—the old form of which was *Aberwick. Berwick* accordingly means the *wick* or town at the mouth of the Tweed. *Car* or *Caer* is the Keltic word for *castle* or *stronghold ;* and we find this name in *Carlisle, Cardiff, Caernarvon,* and others.

(ii) The names of common things which we have received from the Kelts are—*basket, bran, cradle, crockery, clout, cuts* (=*lots*), *darn.* Such words as *button, ribbon, barrel, car,* and *cart,* are also Keltic, but have come into the English language through the Norman-French, who received them from the descendants of the ancient Gauls. Some Keltic words have come to us from Scotland—such as *pony, clan, whisky, claymore* (a kind of sword), *pibroch,* and *plaid ;* and it is chiefly to Sir Walter Scott's writings that we owe the common use of these words. Ireland has also sent us a few Keltic words, such as *Tory, brogue,* and *shamrock.*

21. **THE LATIN ELEMENT OF THE FIRST PERIOD (i).**—The

Roman power, as is generally known, was settled in Britain from the year 43 till the year 410. In the beginning of the year 410, the very existence of the Roman Empire was threatened by the Goths and other warlike peoples ; and the Roman forces were withdrawn to defend the very heart of the empire. The Romans, though conquerors, were true benefactors. They gave the Britons good laws ; cut roads for them through the island ; established camps ; built forts and strongholds ; dug harbours or ports ; and planted military settlements—which they called *colonies*—here and there among the conquered people. When the Romans went away, they left these important benefits behind them ; and, with the things themselves, the words also remained. But they left only six words behind them, and all of these have combined themselves, or gone into composition, with words that are purely English. The following are the six words : Castra, a *camp*; Strata (*via*), a *paved road*; Vallum, a *rampart*; Fossa, a *ditch*; Colonia, a *settlement*; and Portus, a *harbour*.

22. THE LATIN ELEMENT OF THE FIRST PERIOD (ii).—(*a*) The Latin word Castra has become *chester*, *caster*, *cester*, and even *ter* (in *Exeter*). We generally find it in the form of *chester* in the south and west ; *cester* in the middle ; and *caster* in the north and east of England. Thus we have Chester, Manchester, and Winchester in the west and south ; Leicester and Towcester in mid-England ; and Tadcaster, Doncaster, and Lancaster in the north.

(*b*) Strata.—The Romans drove a strongly-built military road from the south-east to the north-west of the island— from Richborough, near Dover, up to the standing camp on the river Dee, which is now called Chester. This was *the* Strata or Street. It was afterwards carried farther north, and even into Scotland. It went right over the crest of a hill in Westmoreland, which is called High Street to this day. We can trace the path of this great military road by the names of the towns and villages that are strung upon it. Thus there are Streatham (near London), Stretton, Stratford-on-Avon, Stony Stratford, Stretford (near Manchester), Stradbroke, and many others.

(c) **Vallum** is found in *wall.*

(d) **Fossa** is found in the names *Fossway, Fosbrooke, Fosbridge,* and others.

(e) **Colonia** is found in *Colne, Colchester, Lincoln,* and others.

(f) **Portus** appears in *Portsmouth, Portsea, Bridport,* and some other names.

23. **THE LATIN ELEMENT OF THE SECOND PERIOD (i).**—This element was not introduced by the Romans themselves, but by Christian missionaries who came from Rome, sent by Pope Gregory the Great to convert, not the Britons, but the English, to Christianity. A band of forty monks, with St Augustine at their head, landed in Kent in the year 597. For four centuries from this date a large number of Latin words came into the English language, chiefly words relating to the church and church observances.

Church Terms.—*Calic,* from *calix,* a cup ; *cluster,* from *claustrum,* a closed place ; *priest,* from *presbyter,* an elder ; *sanct,* from *sanctus,* a holy man ; *sacrament,* from *sacramentum,* a sacred oath ; *predician,* from *prædicare,* to declare ; *regul,* from *regula,* a straight piece of wood. But the old form of most of these words has disappeared, to make room for Norman-French forms from the same Latin source. Along with these were adopted a few Greek words—such as *bishop,* from *episkopos,* an overseer ; *angel,* from *anggelos,* a messenger ; *apostle,* from *apostolos,* a person sent ; *monk,* from *monăchos,** a person who lives alone ; and a few others.

24. **THE LATIN ELEMENT OF THE SECOND PERIOD (ii).**—The introduction of Christianity proved to be the beginning of an intercourse with Rome, Italy, and the Continent ; and this intercourse brought with it commerce. Commerce imported many new things ; and the names of these things came into the island along with the things themselves. Thus we have *butter* from *butyrum ; cheese* from *caseus ;* and *tunic* from *tunica.* We have also *fig* from *ficus ; pear* from *pirum ; lettuce* from *lactuca,* which itself comes from *lac*—milk (and hence means *the milky plant*) ; and *pease* from *pisum.*

* The same root exists in *monarch,* a person who rules alone.

(*Pease* is really the singular ; and *pea* is a false singular—not a plural.) We have also from the same source some names of animals. Such are *camel* from *camēlus; lion* from *leo; oyster* from *ostrea; trout* from *trutta*. A few miscellaneous words have also come to us from this quarter—such as *pound* from the Latin *pondus*, a weight; *candle* from *candēla;* and *table* from *tabŭla*. The Latin word *uncia*, which means the twelfth part of anything, is, as it were, split up into two—and gives the two words *inch* and *ounce*, which are fundamentally but two forms of one word. (But with regard to this class of words also it should be observed that the words directly introduced from the Latin have either been greatly changed in form; or they have been subsequently borrowed again from the French.)

25. THE SCANDINAVIAN ELEMENT (i).—In the year 787, the Northmen, Norsemen, or Normans of Scandinavia, began to make descents on the east coast of England. These attacks were so dreaded by the English that prayers were regularly used in the churches against them ; and a part of the Litany of the time contained the utterance : 'From the incursions of the Normans, good Lord, deliver us !' These attacks went on for three centuries. In the ninth century, these Danes obtained a permanent footing in the northern and eastern parts of England ; and by the eleventh century they had become so strong that Danish kings sat upon the throne of England from 1016 to 1042. These Norsemen were Teutons. They were Teutons who had migrated to the north. As northern people generally do, they preferred hard sounds to aspirates. They preferred a *k* to a *ch; a p* to an *f.* The probable reason is that, in the cold mists of the north, they had learned not to open too much their mouths and throats ; and thus they formed the habit of using a shut sound like *k* to a sound like *ch* (in *loch*), which requires a stream of air to be passed through the throat. We must not forget that it was the *spoken* language of England that was affected by the Danes ; not the *written* language ; for the simple reason that, in these times, not more than one man in a thousand— either among Danes or Englishmen—could read and write.

26. THE SCANDINAVIAN ELEMENT (ii).—The Danish contribution is, like the Keltic, of two kinds : (*a*) Names of places ; and (*b*) Common words.

(*a*) The most remarkable example of the place-name is the noun *by*, which means *town*. There are in England more than six hundred names ending in *by*. Almost all of these lie to the north and east of Watling Street ; to the south of it, there is scarcely one. Thus we have *Whitby*, the *White Town; Tenby*, in Wales, *Dane's town; and Grimsby, the town of Grim*. We find the word *by* also in the compound *by-law*. The following words are also derived from the Danes :

Thorpe, a village...............Althorpe (old); Bishopsthorpe ; Burn- (*Drup* in Jutland, where ham-Thorpe (where Nelson was born). there are scores of towns with this ending.)	
Fell, a hill or table-land......Scawfell, Crossfell, Goat Fell.	
Dale, a valley....................Ribblesdale, Grimsdale.	
Thwaite, a forest clearing....Applethwaite.	
Toft, a homestead...............Lowestoft (the form in Normandy is *tôt*).	
Wick, a creek or bay..........Ipswich, Greenwich, Berwick. (Viking = a creeker.)	
Oe or ea, an island..............Faroe, Chelsea (= *chesel ea*, the shingle island).	
Ness, a nose or cape............Sheerness, Caithness, Fife Ness ; the Naze (in Essex, etc.).	

(*b*) To the Norsemen we also owe the words *are*, which pushed out the pure English *syndon; talk; tarn; busk* (dress) ; *sky; hustings; fellow; odd; blunt; kid;* and many more.

27. THE SCANDINAVIAN ELEMENT (iii).—One result of this mixture of Danes with Englishmen was that both, in trying to speak the language or to use the words of each other, would naturally take firm hold of the *root* of the word, and allow the inflections to take care of themselves. Hence English words would lose their inflections ; and this process, after it had once begun, would go on at an increased speed, the greater became the communication at church and at market between the English and the Danes. The same process is now going on in the United States. Thousands upon thousands of Germans have settled there among an English-speaking people. These Germans are rapidly falling into the habit of using their German words without inflections at all.

28. **LATIN ELEMENT OF THE THIRD PERIOD** (i).—This element is really Norman-French. French is Latin, with many of the inflections lost or changed, and with the pronunciation of the vowel-sounds enormously altered. But it did not come from the written Latin of books; but from the spoken Latin of soldiers and country-people (the *lingua Romana rustica*). Norman-French is the French spoken by the Normans, who lost their own Norsk or Danish speech, and learned French from their French wives and children. In the year 912, the Normans, under Duke Rolf or Rollo, wrested from King Charles the Simple the beautiful valley of the Seine, which was afterwards called by the name of Normandy. Norman-French was a dialect of French, and it differed in many respects from the French spoken in the other parts of France. This Norman-French was introduced into England as a court language by Edward the Confessor, in the year 1042; but it was brought into this country as a folk-speech by bands of Norman-French under the leadership of Duke William, the seventh Duke of Normandy, in the famous year 1066. This Norman-French, which they brought with them, became in England the language of the ruling classes, of the court, of the lawyers, and of all priests high in the ranks of the church. Books ceased to be written in English; boys translated their Latin into French; an English churl had to employ a lawyer who used only French in his law-papers and his pleadings; and even 'uplandish' or country people tried 'to speak Frensch, for to be more ytold of.' The saturation of English with French words probably reached its highest point at the end of the fourteenth century; and about that time a re-action set in. As has been before pointed out, in 1349, boys were allowed to translate their Latin into English; in 1362, Edward III. passed an act of parliament to authorise the use

of English in courts of law ; and even the Normans who lived in London had begun to use English in their families. But, by the time French had ceased to be the language of the upper classes, several thousand French words had found their way into our vocabulary, which had become to a large extent *bilingual.**

29. NORMAN-FRENCH (ii).—The words which have been introduced into our pure English speech from the Normans fall easily into classes.

(*a*) **Feudalism† and War.**—Armour, chivalry, captain, battle, duke, fealty, realm.

The English word for *armour* was *harness ;* and Macaulay uses *harness* in this sense in one of his *Lays :*

> Now while the three were tightening
> Their harness on their backs.

—*Chivalry* comes from the Fr. *cheval*, which is a broken-down form of the Low Latin word *caballus*, a horse.—*Captain* comes from the Lat. *caput*, a head.—*Battle* comes from the Fr. *battre*, to beat.—*Duke* comes from the Fr. *duc*—which comes from the Lat. *dux* (accusative *ducem*, most French nouns being borrowed from the accusative, not the nominative form of the Latin noun), a leader.—*Fealty* is the Norman-French form of the word *fidelity*, from the Lat. *fidelitas*, faithfulness.—*Real-m* is the noun from the adjective *real*, which comes from Lat. *regal-is;* it is the land ruled over by a *rex* or *ré* (a king).

30. (*b*) **Hunting.**—Forest, leveret, quarry, couple, venison.

Forest comes from the Low Lat.‡ *foresta;* from Lat. *foris*, out-of-doors. A forest does not necessarily contain trees ; it is merely the name for the *open* hunting-ground as contrasted with the inclosed space called a park.—

---

* Two-languaged.

† What is called *the feudal system* was based upon war. A knight held land of his baron ; a baron of his king—on condition of bringing so many men into the field on the summons of his overlord.

‡ *Low Latin* is the name for that kind of corruption of Latin which was written and spoken after the breaking up of the Roman Empire in the fifth century.

Leveret, a young hare, from the Fr. *lièvre*; from the Lat. *lepus* (-*oris*).—*Quarry* comes from the Lat. *cor*, the heart, and at first meant the heart and intestines, which were thrown to the dogs who hunted down the wild beast. Milton has the phrase, 'scents his quarry from afar.'—*Couple* comes from the Lat. *copula*, a band.—*Venison* means *hunted flesh*, and comes from the Fr. *venaison*, which comes from the Lat. verb *venari*, to hunt.

31. (*c*) **Cookery.**—Beef, veal, pork, mutton, pullet.

The Saxon hind had the charge of the cattle and animals on the farm while they were alive; but he never saw anything of them after they were killed. He never met them at dinner. The flesh of these animals received French names from the Norman-Frenchmen who ate them; and their Saxon or English names were forgotten. A German says *calf's flesh*, but we use the Norman-French word *veal*. Thus the corresponding English words to those printed above are *ox*, *calf*, *swine*, *sheep*, and *fowl*. The word *beef* comes from the Fr. *bœuf*, which comes from the Lat. *bos* (acc. *bovem*), an ox.—*Veal* comes from the old French word *veel*, which comes from the Lat. *vitellus*, a little calf.—*Pork* comes from Fr. *porc*, which is derived from the Lat. *porcus*, a pig.—*Mutton* comes from the Fr. *mouton*, from the Low Latin word *multo*, a sheep.—*Pullet* comes from Fr. *poulet*, which comes from the Low Latin word *pulla*, a hen.

32. (*d*) **Law.**—Chancellor, judge, parliament, court, assize, sue, damages, and many others.

The word *chancellor* comes from the Fr. *chancelier*; from the Lat. *cancellarius*, the keeper of written papers. 'The officer who had the care of the records stood behind the screen of lattice-work or of cross-bars which fenced off the judgment-seat.' *Cancer* is the Latin name for a crab; *cancellus* is a little crab; *cancelli* are cross-bars or lattice-work, like the claws of crabs crossed. Hence also to *cancel*, which means to draw cross strokes through writing.—*Judge* comes from the French word *juge*, which comes from the Lat. *judex* (= *jus-dic-s*, a sayer of right). The old English term was *dempster*, from the verb *deem;* noun, *doom.—Parliament* comes from the Fr. *parler,* to speak ; from Low Lat. *parabolāre,* to talk ; whence also *parlour,* a room for speaking in.—*Court* comes from the old Fr. *cort;* from Lat. *cohors* or *cors,* an inclosed space. A *cohors* was a sheep-pen ; but it was afterwards applied to a number of soldiers.—*Assize* comes from the old Fr. *assise,* an assembly of judges ; from the Lat. *assidēre,* to sit beside.—*Sue* comes from the old Fr. *suir* (modern Fr. *suivre*) ; from the Lat. *sequi,* to follow. We have from the same root the words *suit, suite, pursue, ensue, issue.—Damages,* from the old Fr. *damáge,* which comes from the Low Lat. *damnaticum,* harm ; which comes from the Lat. *damnum,* loss.

33. (*e*) **Church.**—Friar, relic, tonsure, ceremony, etc.

Friar is a word which comes from the old Fr. *freire,* which is derived from the Lat. *frater,* a brother.—*Relic,* chiefly used in the plural, from Fr. *reliques;* from Lat. *reliquiæ,* remains.—*Tonsure* comes from the Fr. *tonsure;* from Lat. *tonsura,* a cutting.—*Ceremony,* from the Fr. *cérémonie,* a rite ; from Lat. *cærimonia.*

34. **SYNONYMS GIVEN US BY NORMAN-FRENCH.**—Among other benefits which we have received from the coming in of Norman-French into our language, is a number of synonyms.* These have enabled us to give a different shade or colouring to certain words, or to put them to a special use. Thus we speak of the *blessing* of God, and the *benediction* of a clergyman ; of the *bloom* on a peach, and the *flower* of a lily ; of a person as a *member* of a learned society, but not a *limb.* Now *blessing, bloom,* and *limb* are all English ; *benediction, flower,* and *member* are all Latin words—Latin words which have come to us through the doorway of the French language. The following are some more of these synonyms ; and, after examining them, it will generally be found that the English

---

* A *synonym* is a word that has the *same meaning* as another word ; like *begin* and *commence; will* and *testament.* There are very few real synonyms in English ; because when the language acquired a word of similar meaning, it at once set to work to use it in a different *way,* or to give it a different *function,* or to bestow on it a different tone, colouring, or shade.

words are stronger, simpler, and more homely than the French words.

ENGLISH.	FRENCH.	ENGLISH.	FRENCH.
Bough	Branch.	Meal	Flour.
Buy	Purchase.	Mild	Gentle.
Feeling	Sentiment.	Wish	Desire.
Friendly	Amiable.	Work	Labour.
Hearty	Cordial.	Wretched	Miserable.
Luck	Fortune.	Wright	Carpenter.

35. BILINGUALISM.—During the three centuries which lay between 1066 and 1362, the English and the Normans had to meet each other constantly in the field, in the church, at markets, and in towns and villages. They had to buy and sell from each other ; to give and take orders from and to each other ; and to speak with each other on many kinds of business. They also intermarried. Thus the Norman got slowly into the habit of joining an English word with his French word—so as to make it clear to the Englishman ; while the Englishman, on his side, joined the corresponding French word—when he happened to know it—to the English word he had to employ. These words, ever after, ran in couples ; and this habit of going in couples became a habit of the language. Hence it is that, in the opening words of our Prayer-Book, we use such couples as *assemble* and *meet together; acknowledge* and *confess; dissemble* and *cloak;* and *humble* and *lowly.* The words *meet together, acknowledge, cloak,* and *lowly,* represent the purely English part of the congregation ; while the Norman-French supplies such words as *assemble, confess, dissemble,* and *humble.* The great poet of the fourteenth century—Chaucer—has hundreds of examples of such phrases. He gives us, for example, *hunting* and *venerye; mirth* and *jollity; care* and *heed; swinke* and *labour; pray* and *beseech;* a *wright* and *carpenter.* The practice of using these pairs of words has very greatly diminished in our day ; but a few examples still keep their place in the language. Such are *will and testament, use and wont, aid and abet,* and several others.

36. DOUBLETS.—It is chiefly to the same Norman-French influence that we owe a minor phenomenon of the language —the appearance of two forms of the same word. These two forms are called **doublets**. The Norman-French could not pronounce our semi-vowel *w*. They had either to make a *v* of it, or a hard *g*. They preferred the hard *g*; and, to keep it hard, they added a *u*. Thus, for *wile*, they said *guile*; for *wise* (= *manner*), they said *guise*; for *ward, guard*; for *warden, guardian*; for *wardrobe, garderobe*; for *warrant, guarantee*; and so on.

37. DOUBLETS FROM DIALECTS AND OTHER SOURCES.— Besides the doublets due to Norman-French influences, there are many interesting cases which may be referred to. Some are evidently due to differences of dialect. The English language grew up from different centres, which had little or no connection with each other, on account of the difficulties of travelling. Hence a word would take different forms in different dialects—like *church* in the south of the English-speaking country, and *kirk* in the north ; so also with *cole*, of which the northern form is *kail*. Sometimes one word is merely a later and modified form of another, as *draw* of *drag*. In all cases doublets are forms of the same word, which have come through different experiences of place, or time, or other influence. In short, they should be recognised as really one word, with a difference in spelling and meaning, resulting from its history. Other specimens of doublets are *down* and *dune; shriek* and *screech; shell* and *scale; wagon* and *wain*.

38. PRONUNCIATION.—The Norman-French refined our mode of speaking ; made the existing vowel-sounds less coarse ; gave us some new vowel-sounds ; and, above all, taught us to give up most of our rough throat-sounds or gutturals. They gradually turned out the gutturals from the beginning of words ; and *genoh* became *enough*, and *gif, if*. They turned them out of the middle of words ; and *nagel* became *nail*, and *hagel, hail*. They got rid of them at the ends of words ; and we no longer pronounce the guttural in *flight, might, right*, and *sight*. This is all the more absurd and remarkable that we write *the sound that once was there* with two strong gutturals, *g* and *h*. Sometimes the influence of the Norman-French was to turn the guttural into a kind of hissing sound or sibilant ; and it is in this way that we came to say *teach, beseech,* and *catch.* But the *ch* in these words comes back to its older use, and becomes a *gh* again, in the past tense—in *taught, besought,* and *caught.*

39. **LATIN OF THE FOURTH PERIOD.**—The Latin introduced into our language by the Norman-French was a *spoken* Latin. It was the Latin of the *ear and mouth.* It was the everyday speech of the people ; and underwent very great change. The Latin introduced into our language by learned men was a *written* or *printed* Latin. It was the Latin of the *eye and pen.* This Latin is called the *Latin of the Fourth Period;* and it was brought into our language by a powerful movement known as the **Revival of Learning.**—When the Turks took Constantinople in 1453, the learned Greeks of that capital fled from the city, carrying with them their precious manuscript copies of Greek and Latin writers. They fled into Italy, into Germany, and into France and England. They taught Greek and Latin in the universities of these countries ; and very soon the study of Greek and Latin became the fashion among all persons of leisure ; and the stores of thought and beauty in Homer and Sophocles, in Virgil and Horace, were diligently studied and appropriated. Queen Elizabeth was a good Greek scholar, and could both speak and write good Latin. Now began to come into our language thousands of Latin words ; until, in the beginning of the seventeenth century, an eminent writer complains that Englishmen will have ' to learn Latin to understand English, and a work will prove of equal facility in either.' Unlike the Latin words of the Third Period, the Latin words introduced in the sixteenth and seventeenth centuries suffered little or no change. They were transferred from Latin books just as they were—by the accurate aid of the hand and eye, and underwent no process of change or corruption. The Latin *opinio* became *opinion; notio, notion; suggestio, suggestion; separatum, separate; iteratum, iterate;* and so on. It would be a great mistake,

however, to suppose that all the Latin of this *Fourth Period*
came *directly* from the Latin. Most of it came through the
medium of French, as did the Latin of the *Third Period;* but
unlike it, it was not the language of the people. In French,
as in English, it was the language merely of books, of the
literary and of learned men.—It is worthy of notice that
many words which we use every day, and which we think
must *always* have been in the language, only came in about
this period, and are therefore comparatively new. Thus Mr
Gill, the high-master of St Paul's School in 1619, and the
teacher of John Milton in his boyhood, complains of the
introduction of words which are now quite common to all of
us. He says: 'O harsh lips! I now hear all around me
such words as *common, vices, envy, malice;* even *virtue, study,
justice, pity, mercy, compassion, profit, commodity, colour, grace,
favour, acceptance.*' The wonder nowadays would be how
we could possibly get on without these words, and how we
could ever have done without them.

40. MOUTH LATIN AND BOOK LATIN.—The introduction of
Latin words into our English speech by two doors—by the
living conversation of living people, and by the silent door
of books, has given rise to a phenomenon of the same kind
as that described in section 36. But the phenomenon of
duplicates or doublets presents itself to our notice on a much
larger scale now ; and, in every case, the duplicate word
becomes in reality two separate words—employed for separate
purposes, and with perfectly distinct meanings. Thus,
though *legal, leal,* and *loyal* are, in their origin, fundamentally
the same word, their meanings are perfectly distinct and
even widely different ; *hospital* and *hotel* are the same words,
but they are no longer used in the same sense ; while *fact*
and *feat* have also widely diverged from each other in use
and in signification. The Latin words that have come
from the Latin language by the path of books, have kept
their Latin shape, and may be called *Book Latin.* The
Latin words that have come to us by the path of Norman-
French have undergone great alterations ; and they may
be called *spoken Latin.* The chief process of alteration

undergone by them is that of *squeezing*; three syllables have generally been squeezed into two. The following is a list:

DUPLICATE WORDS OR DOUBLETS.

LATIN.	BOOK LATIN.	SPOKEN LATIN.
Benedictio,	benediction,	benison.
Cadentia (things falling or befalling),	cadence,	chance.
Captivus,	captive,	caitiff.
Conceptio,	conception,	conceit.
Cophinus,	coffin,	coffer.
Debitum,	debit,	debt.
Defectum,	defect,	defeat.
Dilatare,	dilate,	delay.
Exemplum,	example,	sample.
Fabrica,	fabric,	forge.
Factio,	faction,	fashion.
Factum,	fact,	feat.
Fidelitas,	fidelity,	fealty.
Fragilis,	fragile,	frail.
Gentilis,	gentile,	gentle, genteel.
Granum (a grain),	granary,	garner.
Historia,	history,	story.
Hospitale,	hospital,	hotel.
Lectio,	lection,	lesson.
Legalis,	legal,	loyal.
Major (greater),	major,	mayor.
Maledictio,	malediction,	malison.
Nutrimentum,	nutriment,	nourishment.
Oratio,	oration.	orison.
Pagus (a country district or canton),	pagan,	paynim (the heathen).
Particula,	particle,	parcel.
Pauper,	pauper,	poor.
Penitentia,	penitence,	penance.
Persecutum,	persecute,	pursue.
Potio (a draught),	potion,	poison.
Providentia,	providence,	prudence.
Pungens,	pungent,	poignant.
Quietus,	quiet,	coy.
Radius,	radius,	ray.
Regalis,	regal,	royal.
Respectus,	respect,	respite.
Securus,	secure,	sure.

LATIN.	BOOK LATIN.	SPOKEN LATIN.
Senior,	senior,	sir.
Separatum,	separate,	sever.
Species,	species,	spices.
Status,	state,	estate.
Superficies,	superficies,	surface.
Tractus,	tract,	trait, treat.
Traditio (a giving up),	tradition,	treason.

NOTES.—*Benison* is the opposite of *malison*. A *caitiff* was a person who *allowed* himself to be taken captive. A *feat of arms* was a *fact* or *deed of arms*; hence a *feat* par excellence. The hard guttural *c* in *fabric* has become a sibilant *g* in *forge*, by Nor. Fr. influence. The *g* in *fragile* was originally hard. *Major* is a *greater captain*: a *mayor* is a *greater alderman*. *Orison* may be compared with *benison, poison, reason,* and *treason*. The *p* in *separate* has become a *v* in *sever*; both letters being *labials*. The cutting down of the five syllables in *superficies* into two in *surface*, is the most remarkable instance of compression in the whole list.

Many of the Book Latin words in the above list, such as captive, debit, defect, fact, &c., were borrowed directly from the Latin, and not through the medium of French books.

41. GREEK DOUBLETS.—The same phenomenon has also taken place with reference to Greek words. It is of course the newer form of these words that was given us by the revival of learning; the older forms may have existed in the language since the coming of Augustine in the end of the sixth century.

GREEK.	OLDER FORM.	NEWER FORM.
Adamas,	adamant,	diamond.
Asphodĕlos,	asphodel,	daffodil.
Balsamon,	balsam,	balm.
Blasphemein,	blaspheme,	blame.
Cheirourgos,	chirurgeon,	surgeon.
Dactŭlos (a finger),	date (the fruit),	dactyl.
Phantasia,	fancy,	phantasy.
Phantasma,	phantasm,	phantasy.
Presbutĕros,	priest,	presbyter.
Paralysis,	palsy,	paralysis.
Scandalon,	slander,	scandal.

NOTES.—*Adamant* means *the unsubduable*: a *chirurgeon* is literally a *worker with the hand*: *phantasia* is the power of *presenting to the mind's eye* a bodily image that is not present; *presbuteros* means simply *elder*. In the time of Shakspeare, *fancy* meant *love*. 'Tell me where is fancy bred!' is the first line of a song in the *Merchant of Venice*.

42. ENGLISH WORDS AND FRENCH WORDS IN SENTENCES.—
The difference between English steeped in French and Latin,
and English written almost wholly in pure English words,
can be at once seen in the two following passages, which are
taken from the work of Mr C. Schele De Vere, an American
writer.

(a) 'The Norman *altered* and *increased* our *language*; but
he could not *extirpate* it. To *defend* his *conquest*, he took
possession of the *country*; and, *master* of the *soil*, he *erected*
fortresses and *castles*, and *attempted* to *introduce* new *terms*.
The *universe* and the *firmament*—the *planets*, *comets*, and
meteors—the *atmosphere* and the *seasons*, all were *impressed*
with the *seal* of the *conqueror*. Hills became *mountains*, and
dales *valleys*; streams were called *rivers*, and brooks *rivulets*;
waterfalls, *cascades*; and woods, *forests*.'

All the words in italics in the above passage are either of
Latin or of French origin; if of French, then they are Latin
at second-hand.

(b) 'But the *dominion* of the Norman did not *extend* to the
home of the Englishman, it stopped at the threshold of his
house; there, around the fireside in his kitchen,* and the
hearth in his room,* he met his beloved kindred; the bride,
the wife, and the husband, sons and daughters, brothers and
sisters, tied to each other by love, friendship, and kind feel-
ings, knew nothing dearer than their own sweet home.'

Only one word in the above is French (*dominion*), and two
are Latin (*extend* and *kitchen*). All the others are purely
English.

43. ENGLISH WORDS LOST.—The copious introduction of
Norman-French, Latin, and Greek terms into our language,
had the effect of pushing a great number of purely English
words *out* of our speech, or at least of making them less
frequent in use. Thus we used to say *fore-elders*, but this
word has had its place taken by *ancestors*; *fairhood* has been
pushed out by *beauty*; and *wonstead* by *residence*. In the same

---

* He might have said *hall* and *bower*. In the old English times, the *hall*
was the outer room of the cottage, into which the front door opened, and
bower was the inner room.

C

way, *forewit* has given place to *caution; licherest** to *cemetery; inwit* to *conscience; bookhoard* to *library;* and *hindersome* to *obstructive.* In fact, it is often easier for us to understand foreign words than those of our own native home-grown speech. The title of an old book written in the thirteenth century is the *Ayenbite†* of *Inwyt*—a title which is to us much more intelligible in its Franco-Latin translation of *Remorse of Conscience.* Mr Barnes, the Dorsetshire poet, has tried to re-introduce the genuine homely English way of speaking and writing ; and to banish Latin terms. Thus, in his *Grammar* or 'Book of Speech-Craft,' he calls *singular, onely; plural, somely ;* and he calls *degrees of comparison, pitches of suchness.* The difficulty he has to contend with is, that this home English is less intelligible to our modern ears than the foreign Latin. Thus the following sentence looks like a word-puzzle : 'These pitch-marks off mark sundry things by their sundry suchnesses, as, "The *taller* or *less tall* man of the two is my friend."' And he also says— what is a useful warning for us : 'Speech was shapen of the breath-sounds of speakers, for the ears of hearers ; and not from speech-tokens (letters) in books, for men's eyes.'

CHAPTER II.

The History of the Grammar of English.

1. AN INFLECTED LANGUAGE.—When, in the fifth century, our English speech was brought over from the Continent, it was a highly inflected or synthetic language ; and it remained in this condition for several centuries. The coming of the Danes had the effect of beginning the dropping off of inflections. The coming of the Normans extended very much and hastened this process, which has gone on with considerable rapidity down to the present day. We may put the general fact in this way :

* A *liche* or *lyke* originally meant *body.*
† *Ayenbite* = *againbite.* The *again* corresponds to the *re* in *remorse.*

The English Language was a **Synthetic Language** down to about the year 1100; since that time, it has been becoming more and more of an **Analytic Language**.

2. **THE GRAMMAR OF NOUNS.**—In the very oldest English—or, as it is commonly called, *Anglo-Saxon*—nouns were declined in different ways, and had several declensions, just as German and Latin have. Each of these declensions had four cases. Nowadays we have only one declension and only one inflection for the cases of nouns. That one inflection is 's for the possessive case. The following is an example of an old declension :

DECLENSION OF **EAGE**, THE EYE.

	Sing.	Plur.		Sing.	Plur.
Nom	Eage (eye).	Eagan.	*Dat*	Eag-an (to).	Eag-um.
Pos	Eag-an (of).	Eag-ena.	*Obj*	Eage.	Eagan.

Again, in this English, gender did not follow sex, but was poetic and fantastic. *Tongue* and *week* were feminine nouns, as they still are in modern German ; *star* and *sea*, masculine ; *wife* and *child*, neuter.—In old English there were a great many plural endings, as –**as, –an, –u, –a, –o.** After the Norman Conquest they were greatly reduced, **es** or –**s** being now the ordinary ending, –**en** being exceptional.

3. **THE GRAMMAR OF ADJECTIVES.** — Adjectives had also cases. Adjectives had four cases, three genders, and two numbers. Now we say *good* for all cases, genders, and numbers. In the fourteenth century the only ending which adjectives possessed was **e** for the plural. Thus Chaucer (1340–1400) writes of the little birds :

And *smalë* fowlës maken melodie.

4. **GRAMMAR OF DEFINITE ARTICLE.**—This article was declined like an adjective, in three different genders. Now it has no inflections at all. It has still, however, a clear and distinct memory of one case, which survives in such phrases as, 'The more, the merrier.' This sentence might be written, 'þy̌ more, þy̌ merrier.' That is to say, 'By that more, by that merrier.' The measure of the increase of the company is the measure of the increase of the merriment.

5. GRAMMAR OF THE PERSONAL PRONOUN.—The personal pronoun was also highly inflected in the oldest English ; and the two personal pronouns of the first and second persons possessed this remarkable peculiarity, that it had three numbers, singular, dual, and plural. The dual form stood for *We two* and for *You two;* and, if we cared to trouble ourselves nowadays with a host of inflections, these would certainly be very convenient.

All this is now very much changed. The dual number is completely gone ; the use of *thou*, except in religious compositions, has been given up, and the true possessive of *it*, which is **his**, has given place to the incorrect form *its*. The possessive *its* is very seldom found in Shakspeare, and there is only one instance of it in our present translation of the Bible : 'That which groweth of its own accord of thy harvest thou shalt not reap' (Lev. xxv. 5). But another reading is, 'of it own accord.'

6. GRAMMAR OF VERBS.—The verb possessed also, in the oldest times, before the language was at all influenced by Norman-French, a large number of inflections. At the present time a verb has only five inflections ; but, if it belongs to the strong conjugation, it may have six. Let us look at the old verb *niman*, to take, which still survives in our adjective *nimble*, which means *quick at taking*.

The chief tenses of **niman** were inflected as follows :

PRESENT TENSE.		PAST TENSE.	
Sing.	*Plural.*	*Sing.*	*Plural.*
1. nime.	nimath.	1. nám.	námon.
2. nimest.	nimath.	2. náme.	námon.
3. nimeth.	nimath.	3. nám.	námon.

Of all the inflections in the above, only two still remain, *st* in the second person singular, and *th* in the third person ; and even these two inflections are nowadays hardly used at all.

7. FRAGMENTS OF NOUN INFLECTIONS.—Although our language, in the course of its history, has lost almost all of its inflections, there still remain, here and there, in our grammar, fragments of inflections which are often curiously disguised, and therefore difficult to recognise. Thus, at first sight, it is not easy to see that *vixen* is the feminine of *fox*. But *vixen* is simply the same as *fixen*, or *fyxen*, and it was one of the laws of Anglo-Saxon vowel-change that *o* became *y*. It was very usual to make the plural of nouns in *en*. Thus we said *shoon*, *hosen*, *tren*, *been* (for *bees*), *toon* (for *toes*), *flon* (for *arrows*), and *fleen* (for *fleas*). But, of all these and other similar plurals, we now possess only one—*oxen*. The plurals *children* and *brethren* are really double plurals. The oldest plurals were *cildru*, afterwards *childer*; and *brether*. It was then forgotten that these were real plurals, and an *en* was added.

8. FRAGMENTS OF ADJECTIVE INFLECTIONS.—We have the comparative *rather* (rightly pronounced in Ireland *rayther*); but we have no *rathe* or *rathest*. An old writer, speaking of a star, says : ' It rose rather and rather (earlier).' Nighest becomes *next*; because the **g** + **s** is equal to an **x**. So there was in our country an old proverb, 'When bale is hext, bone is next'—that is, ' When evil is highest, boon is nighest.' *Over* is now only used as a preposition. But it is really the comparative degree of the old adjective *ov*, which is a form of *up* or *off*.

9. FRAGMENTS OF PRONOUN INFLECTIONS.—The *t* in *it* (which was formerly *hit*, as the neuter of *he*) is simply the sign of the neuter gender, and is the same *t* that is found in *tha-t*, *wha-t* (the neuter of *who*), etc. Hence the true possessive of *it* is *his;* and this is the form in use in Shakspeare and Bacon, and even down to the middle of the seventeenth century. *Its*, as we have already seen, is a blunder. *They* is not the true plural of *he;* but really of the old definite article *thaet*.

10. FRAGMENTS OF VERB INFLECTIONS.—The inflections of the verb are very strangely disguised ; and, if learned men had not worked hard, and made diligent inquiry in many directions, we should never have known what they really are. Thus the *m* in *am* is the same *m* that is found in *me;* and the oldest form known of the verb *am*, in the oldest language, is *asmi*.—The *t* which we find in the second person of some

verbs, such as *art, wast, shalt,* and *wilt,* is the same as the *th*
in *thou.* This *t* is therefore the pronoun *thou* added to the
verb.—The *th* in the old-fashioned third person singular
writeth, hopeth, etc., is the same *th* that we find in *the* and
that. Accordingly, we may say that *burneth* is = *that (thing)
burns.*—The last *d* in *did* is not the same as the *ed* in *walked.
Did* is not = *doed.* An older form of *did* is *dude;* and from
this we see that the past tense was formed by doubling the
present—by reduplication. Thus we see that it is the last *d*
that represents the *do.*—The word *worth* in the well-known
lines from the *Lady of the Lake*—

> Woe worth the chase, woe worth the day,
> That cost thy life, thou gallant gray!—

is not an adjective, but the remnant of an old verb. This
verb is *weorthan,* to become ; and *worth* is the imperative of it.
When a verb has lost one of its parts, it goes to another verb,
and borrows the use of one of its parts. Thus *went,* the past
tense of *go,* is borrowed from *wend.*

11. FRAGMENTS OF INFLECTIONS IN ADVERBS.—Adverbs
contain a great number of disguised inflections. In the
present day, we make adverbs from adjectives by adding *ly*
to them—as *neat, neatly ; warm, warmly.* But, in old English,
the adverb was made by employing the dative of the adjective. Thus, *brightē* was = *in a bright manner ; swiftē* was =
swiftly. Then *ē* very soon dropped off; and the word was
left in its bare root—stripped of inflections. And so it has
happened that we have many adverbs which are used in their
simplest form, and are just the same as adjectives. We do
not say, 'He runs fastly,' but 'He runs fast ;' 'He works
hardly,' but 'He works hard.'—But the remnants of other
cases are also found in adverbs. Thus *needs, always, sideways, once* (for *onēs*), *twice* (for *twiēs*), *unawares, whence* (for
whennēs) and others, are all old possessives.—*Seldom* is an old
dative plural. *Seld* meant *rare;* and *seldom* means *at rare
times.*—*The* in the phrase, 'The older the better,' is an ablative
or *instrumental* case ; and therefore means *by that.* Accordingly this sentence means : 'By that older, by that better.'

The measure of the increase of age is the measure of the increase of the quality.

12. FRAGMENTS OF INFLECTIONS IN PREPOSITIONS.—*Since* is the possessive case of the old English word *sithen*. The following are the steps: *Sithennés; sithens; sithence; since.—After* is the comparative degree of the old preposition *af* (= of), which meant *from. Over* is another comparative form, from a root which appears in *up*.

CHAPTER III.

Changes in Modern English.

1. FORMATION OF MODERN ENGLISH.—We have seen that the substance of the living English tongue was brought from Germany to this island by our Teutonic ancestors. We have seen also that it has undergone a great variety of influences, the greatest and strongest of which was the Norman Conquest. For a long time after the Conquest, the English language was the tongue of a subject and humiliated race; it ceased to be fashionable, and almost ceased to be literary. In the thirteenth century it began to revive, but with very important changes; the inflections, and many of the old English words, being lost, and a multitude of new words being introduced. In Chaucer's time it regained its old position as the language of the court, of fashion, and of literature. In 1485 we find the language in all important respects fixed as we have it now. Every intelligent Englishman is able to understand all that has since been written.

Modern English, then, dates from 1485, the year when the Wars of the Roses ended with the battle of Bosworth, and the Tudor line ascended the throne. It was the time also when the art of printing was introduced by Caxton; and about the time when the two great events, the Revival of Learning and the Reformation, took place.

2. CONTINUED HISTORY OF OUR LANGUAGE.—It would be a mistake, however, to suppose that the language has

no history after 1485. Language is the expression and embodiment of thought; and as thought varies with the varying experience of man, language must change accordingly. Since 1485 the English people have gone through marvellous changes—changes in political and social life, in science, in art, and industry. They have planted extensive colonies, they carry on trade in every part of the world, and have dealings with every nation. In all this widening and progressive life, we have got to know far more than we did in 1485, and thus require to use a multitude of words unknown to the people of that period. The result has been a large addition to our vocabulary.

3. BORROWING FROM SPANISH AND ITALIAN.—Under the heading 'Latin of the Fourth Period,' we have noted the number of words borrowed from the Latin during the sixteenth century. We are now to observe that about the same time there was a considerable borrowing of words from the Spanish and Italian. Of course, as Italian and Spanish are offshoots from Latin, these words also are mostly of Latin origin.

(i) Italian.—During the sixteenth and seventeenth centuries Italian literature was very extensively studied by English writers. For some centuries the Italians were the most cultivated people in Europe. Italy was the home of music, painting, and sculpture. Her poets served as models to those of other nations. The earliest poets of modern England, such as Wyatt and Surrey, were inspired by them; Spenser and Milton were ardent students of their works. During this period, consequently, we introduced from the Italian language many important words, among which may be mentioned *sonnet, opera, cupola, balcony, palette.*

(ii) Spanish.—At the same time we had even more intimate relations with Spain, though of a different kind. In the sixteenth century Spain was the leading nation of Europe. She had the best soldiers, the first generals and statesmen; her ships discovered America; and her kings aimed at universal dominion. As both friend and enemy, England was brought into close connection with the Spaniards. Under these circumstances we naturally adopted many words from them. While most of these were of Latin origin, not a few related to the new countries discovered and conquered by Spain in America. Among the Spanish words may be mentioned *buffalo, alligator, don, armada, indigo, potato, tobacco.* The last two are of American origin. The rest are Latin. *Alligator* is of Latin origin, but is the name of an American animal.

4. **DUTCH WORDS.**—We have borrowed very few words from the Germans ; but from the people of the Netherlands, who have always been near neighbours to us, we have derived not a few. Long ago, Flemings (or people of Flanders) were settled in Wales and Norfolk. In the reign of Queen Elizabeth, thousands of Protestant refugees from Antwerp and other places in the Netherlands found an asylum in England. Since the rise of Holland we have had many dealings, both warlike and commercial, with the Dutch. All this accounts for the goodly number of Dutch words which we now find in the English language, such as *burgomaster, ballast, holster, trigger, yacht, yawl.*

5. It will have been clearly seen that there are two main elements in the English language—the Teutonic element, which is by far the most important ; and the Latin element. It is interesting to trace the relative proportion of these two elements as used by the great English writers. In the seventeenth century, especially in such writers as Milton and Sir Thomas Browne, we find a large use of the Latin element, accompanied by a Latin or complex and involved structure of sentence. Towards the end of the century, and especially in the beginning of the eighteenth, during the period of Queen Anne, a simpler style prevailed, the classical element being more sparingly used. But as we proceed into the eighteenth century, the Latin part of the language is again more largely employed by such writers as Johnson, Gibbon, and Hume ; and it is again accompanied by a more formal and elaborate structure of sentence. But before the century closes, there is a return to simplicity and naturalness.

6. In the present century there are many influences specially worth noting as affecting the language :

(i) Social and Political Causes.—Society is a complex thing, continually growing. New facts and ideas are perpetually making themselves felt, necessitating new words, or a more extending meaning in old words. In this province, then, changes in language are incessantly required. Hence the need for such new words as *extradition, neutralisation, secularisation;* even for such unhappy coinages as *burke.* On occasion of the great volunteer reviews of 1881, words like *entrain* and *detrain,* applied to troops, could be noticed creeping in. *Closure* and *clôture* were rivals for currency during the debates of 1882; and *Boycott* began to present serious claims to permanent citizenship in the English tongue.

(ii) Popularising of Technical and Scientific Terms.—One of the most marked features of the nineteenth century is the great diffusion of scientific knowledge, and the application of it to the uses of practical life. The highest scientific results are becoming common property ; and the discoveries of science have been made to satisfy the common needs of men. The result is that terms once unknown or exclusively technical have gained the widest currency in the popular speech. There is no need to mention such familiar words as *telegraph, photograph,* or even *telephone* or *photophone.* The old noun *wire* has now established its right to be used as a verb. In other spheres such terms as *objective, subjective, æsthetics,* now fulfil important functions ; *æsthete* also seems too useful a word to be dispensed with.

(iii) Revival of Archaisms.—In many of our recent poets there has been a tendency to revive some of the old Spenserian or Shaksperian words. But as these are purely literary terms, with no currency in the common speech, they need not be dwelt on.

(iv) Introduction of Scotticisms and Americanisms.—The right of the Scottish tongue to be considered one of the worthiest varieties of the genuine old English or Saxon tongue is now generally recognised. But apart from that, the intrinsic merit of such words as *eerie, glamour, sough, bonnie, douce* (both of which last, however, are of French origin), will probably secure them a permanent place in our language. The influence of America will also be more and more felt on the common English language, whether through its stock of old Saxon phrases which have been preserved in America, through the innovations made by its humorists, or the new experiences in its social and political life.

(v) **Further borrowing from Foreign Languages.**—Even the most remote and unlikely make important and familiar contributions to our tongue. From the Malays we have (along with the thing) borrowed the words *bamboo, gong, sago;* from the Australians we have *boomerang* and *kangaroo;* and from South African tongues, *gnu, quagga, kraal.*

CHAPTER IV.

Words adopted from Foreign Languages.

1. **FROM AFRICAN DIALECTS.**— Chimpanzee, gnu, gorilla, karoo, kraal, zebra.
2. **FROM AMERICAN TONGUES.**— Buccaneer, cacique, cannibal, canoe, caoutchouc, cayman, chocolate, condor, guano, hammock, jaguar, jalap, jerked (beef), llama, mahogany, maize, manioc, moccasin, mustang, opossum, pampas, pemmican, potato, skunk, squaw, tapioca, tobacco, tomahawk, tomato, wigwam, yam.
3. **FROM THE ARABIC LANGUAGE.** (The word *al* means *the.* Thus *alcohol = the spirit.* A few of the following words, however, though they have come to us through Arabic, belong originally to other tongues. Thus alchemy and talisman are from the Greek; apricot is Latin.)—Admiral, alchemy, alcohol, alcove, alembic, algebra, alkali, amber, apricot,

arrack, arsenal, artichoke, assassin, assegai, attar, azimuth, azure, caliph, carat, chemistry, cipher, civet, coffee, cotton, crimson, dragoman, elixir, emir, fakir, felucca, gazelle, giraffe, harem, hookah, koran (or alcoran), lute, magazine, mattress, minaret, mohair, monsoon, mosque, mufti, nabob, nadir, naphtha, salaam, senna, sherbet, shrub (the drink), simoom, sirocco, sofa, sultan, syrup, talisman, tamarind, tariff, vizier, zenith, zero.

4. **FROM CHINESE.**—Bohea, congou, hyson, joss, junk, nankeen, pekoe, souchong, tea.
5. **FROM DUTCH** (words relating chiefly to naval affairs).—Boom, boor, hoy, luff, reef, schiedam (gin), skates, skipper, sloop, smack, smuggle, stiver, taffrail, wear (of a ship), yacht.
6. **FROM FRENCH.**—Aide-de-camp,

belle, bivouac, blonde, bouquet, brunette, brusque, carte-de-visite, coup-d'état, débris, début, déjeûner (breakfast), depot, éclat, ennui, etiquette, naive, naïveté, nonchalance, personnel, précis, programme, protégé, recherché, soirée.

7. **FROM GERMAN** (mostly mining terms).—Cobalt, felspar, hornblend, landgrave, loafer, margrave, meerschaum, nickel, plunder, poodle, quartz, zinc.

8. **FROM HEBREW** (words relating chiefly to religion).—Abbey, abbot, amen, behemoth, cabal, cherub, gehenna, hallelujah, hosannah, Jehovah, jubilee, leviathan, manna, paschal, pharisee, pharisaical, rabbi, sabbath, Sadducees, Satan, seraph, shibboleth, Talmud.

9. **FROM HINDU.**—Avatar, banyan, bungalow, calico, chintz, coolie, cowrie, durbar, jungle, lac (of rupees), loot, mulligatawny, pagoda, palanquin, pariah, punch, pundit, rajah, rupee, ryot, sepoy, shampoo, sugar, suttee, thug, toddy.

10. **FROM HUNGARIAN.**—Hussar.

11. **FROM ITALIAN.**—Alarm, alert, alto, bagatelle, balcony, balustrade, bandit, bankrupt, bravo, brigade, brigand, broccoli, burlesque, bust, cameo, canteen, canto, caprice, caricature, carnival, cartoon, cascade, cavalcade, charlatan, citadel, colonnade, concert, contralto, conversazione, cornice, corridor, cupola, curvet, dilettante, ditto, doge, domino, extravaganza, fiasco, folio, fresco, gazette, gondola, granite, grotto, guitar, incognito, influenza, lagoon, lava, lazaretto, macaroni, madonna, madrigal, malaria, manifesto, motto, moustache, niche, opera, oratorio, palette, pantaloon, parapet, pedant, pianoforte, piazza, pistol, portico,

proviso, quarto, regatta, ruffian, serenade, sonnet, soprano, stanza, stiletto, stucco, studio, tenor, terra-cotta, tirade, torso, trombone, umbrella, vermilion, vertu, virtuoso, vista, volcano, zany.

12. **FROM MALAY.**—Amuck, bamboo, bantam, caddy, cockatoo, dugong, gamboge, gong, guttapercha, mandarin (through the Portuguese), mango, ourang-outang, rattan, sago, upas.

13. **FROM PERSIAN.**—Bazaar, bashaw, caravan, check, checkmate, chess, dervish, divan, firman, hazard, horde, houri, jar, jackal, jasmine, lac (a gum), lemon, lilac, lime (the fruit), musk, orange, paradise, pasha, rook, saraband, sash, scimitar, shawl, taffeta, turban.

14. **FROM POLYNESIAN DIALECTS.** —Boomerang, kangaroo, taboo, tattoo (to paint the skin).

15. **FROM PORTUGUESE.**—Albatross, caste, cobra, cocoa-nut, commodore, fetish, lasso, marmalade, moidore, palaver, port (Oporto).

16. **FROM RUSSIAN.**—Czar, drosky, knout, morse (walrus), steppe, ukase.

17. **FROM SPANISH.**—Alligator, armada, barricade, battledore, bravado, buffalo, caracole, cargo, cigar, cochineal, cork, creole, desperado, don, duenna, El dorado, embargo, filibuster (from English flyboat), filigree, flotilla, galleon (a ship), grandee, grenade, guerilla, indigo, jennet, matadore, merino, mosquito, mulatto, negro, octoroon, quadroon, renegade, savannah, sherry (Xeres), tornado, vanilla.

18. **FROM TARTAR.**—Caviare (the roe of the sturgeon).

19. **FROM TURKISH.**—Bey, caftan, chibouk, chouse, janissary, kiosk, odalisque, ottoman, tulip, yashmak, yataghan.

CHIEF DATES IN THE HISTORY OF THE ENGLISH LANGUAGE.

A.D.

1. **Cædmon** wrote a *Paraphrase of the Scriptures* in First English prose..................670

2. **Bede,** or **Bæda,** wrote a translation into English of part of the *Gospel of St John*..................735

3. **King Alfred** translated many Latin works into English, among others, the *Ecclesiastical History of the English Nation.* King Alfred died..................901

4. **Ælfric** translates parts of the Bible..................1000

5. **Anglo-Saxon Chronicle** brought to a stop about..................1154

6. **Normandy** taken from England under King John. Normans now obliged to regard themselves as Englishmen, and more ready to use the English tongue..................1204

7. **Layamon's** *Brut*—a poem—the first English book written after the stoppage of the *Chronicle* (written in the *Southern English* dialect)..................1205

8. **First Proclamation** ever written in English, issued by Henry III..................1258

9. **Sir John Mandeville,** the first writer of *formed* English prose, 'publishes' his *Travels*..................1356
   (*Publishes* in this century means: *Allows copies in manuscript to be made of his book.*)

10. **Edward III.** authorises the use of English instead of French in courts of law and in schools..................1362

11. **John Wicliffe** translates most of the Bible..................1380

12. **Geoffrey Chaucer,** the 'Father of English Poetry,' wrote his *Canterbury Tales* about..................1388

13. **William Caxton** prints the first English book ever printed, *The History of Troyes*, in Flanders..................1471

14. **Caxton** erects the first printing-press in the Broad Sanctuary, in Westminster, and publishes the first book ever printed in England, the *Game and Playe of the Chesse*..................1474

15. **The Book of Common Prayer** compiled by Cranmer..................1549

16. **The English Bible,** based upon William Tyndall's and other translations, published..................1611

CHAPTER V.

Notes on the Growth of English Words.

1. ROOTS; INFLUENCE OF IMITATION ON LANGUAGE.— The question of the origin of language is an extremely interesting one, which has been long and keenly discussed. But it is one on which the opinions of the learned are not agreed, and we cannot dwell upon it here. There is an established fact, however, which is of the highest interest and importance : most of the words of the great family of Indo-European languages can be traced to a few hundred roots ; and these roots are common to the whole family. It is the greatest achievement of philological science to have clearly established this fact. How these roots have originated, is a more uncertain inquiry : in fact, is just the question of the origin of language presented in another form. It is the theory of some that words have arisen from the imitation of natural sounds ; the names of animals for, instance, being imitations of the sounds they utter. Though this has been ridiculed under the nickname of the *bow-wow* theory, there seems to be some truth in it : at anyrate no one will deny that in the English, as in all other languages, a great many words exist which are imitative of natural sounds. Among such words the following may be mentioned : *Babble, boom, chatter, chirp, clang, clatter, clink, crash, croak, cuckoo, fizz, giggle, gurgle, hiss, howl, hum, hush, murmur, quack, scream, shriek, squeal, thud, thump, thwack, twang, whack, wheeze, whirr, whizz.*

Of course these words were not all originally English. *Clang* and *murmur*, for instance, are Latin words ; but they also are of imitative origin.

2. HYBRIDS.—A *hybrid* is a word composed of a *mixture* of foreign and native elements. Sometimes an English word has a Latin ending ; sometimes a Latin word has an English

ending. All such words are called *hybrids*. One of the most interesting of the earliest hybrids in English was the word *bondage*, which is said to have been introduced in the year 1303. The word *bond* comes to us from the Icelandic or Norwegian word *bondi*, which means *farmer* or *tiller of the soil*. Farmers in Norway are to this day called *bonders*. The suffix *age* is Latin ; but it has come to us through Norman-French. The full Latin ending is *atĭcum*, which, in France, in the course of generations, was compressed into *age*. There are other hybrids with this ending, such as *tillage* (which has pushed out the pure English *tilth*), *cartage*, *stowage*, and others.—The ending *able*, which comes to us from Latin, combines very easily with words which are purely English. Thus we have *lovable*, *biddable*, *laughable*, *breakable*, and others.— The Latin ending *osus* means *full of*. Thus, *vinum* is *wine*, and *vinosus* is *full of wine*. This *ōsus* becomes in English *ous ;* and we find this Latin suffix added to words which are purely English. Thus we have *wondrous* from *wonder*, and *ravenous* from *raven*. We have also *righteous*, which was originally *rightwis*, and the change into *righteous* was a corruption of the spelling.—*Dis* is a Latin prefix, and it is added to English words. Thus we have *dislike* and *disown*. We have also *dishearten*, an old word, in which the prefix *dis* contradicts the suffix *en* (which means *to put* or *make*).—*Re*, another Latin prefix, unites with purely English words, and we find *renew*, *reopen*, *rebuild*, *reclothe*, and others.—French words with English prefixes are also found. Thus we have *besiege ;* the word *siege*, a *seat*, being French. *To besiege* means to take a seat in front of a town, with your mind made up not to go till you have taken it.—Latin words with English endings are found in *useful*, *useless*, *usefulness*, *uselessness*, and others. English words with Latin or French endings are not uncommon. Thus we have *goddess*, *forbearance*, *hindrance*, *oddity*, and others. In old-fashioned English, and even in Wordsworth, who died in 1850, we find such curious formations as *oddments*, *needments*, *eggments* (*eggings on* or *incitements*), and a few others.

3. WORDS DISGUISED IN FORM OR IN MEANING.

Abase, to bring or make low. From a Low Latin word *bassus*, low.

Abate, to *beat* down. Low Lat. *abbattère.*

Adder, O. E. *nadder.* The *n* has dropped from the noun, owing to the mistaken notion that it belonged to the article. Compare umpire for numpire (*non par*—that is, *not equal*), orange for norange (Pers. *nâranj*), apron for napron. The dropping of the *n* is probably owing to the prefixing of *an* and *mine.*

Adrift, on or in the *drift.* From the verb *drive.* Compare *give, gift; shrive, shrift.*

Alligator is Spanish *el* lagarto, *the* lizard (*par excellence*), from Lat. *lacerta,* a lizard.

Aloft, on-loft, in the lift (air). Northern Eng. or 'Scotch' *lift,* the air.

Anon, *on* or *in-one* (instant). The phrase *then ones* has become *the nonce.*

Atonement, *at-one-ment;* bringing into one, reconciliation. In *alone* and *atone* the numeral *one* has its true sound.

Babble, to keep saying *ba, ba.*

Balloon, a large *ball* (Fr.). The *oon* is augmentative.

Ballot, a little *ball* (Fr.). The *ot* is diminutive.

Bank, a *bench* on which money is laid out.

Batch, the quantity of bread *baked* at one time. Compare *wake, watch.*

Bird, one of a *brood* (formerly *brid*). Compare *three, third; burn, brand; work, wright.* In all these the *r* changes its place.

Bran-new, that is, *brand-new,* burnt-new, as if newly from the fire.

Breakfast, a *breaking* of a *fast.* Compare Fr. *déjeûner,* from *jeûne.*

Brick, a piece *broken* off.

Brimstone, that is, *burn-stone,* from *brennan,* to burn. Compare *brindled.* The *r* is a letter which is easily moved. Compare *three* and *third; burn* and *brown;* etc.

Brood, something *bred.*

Butcher, O. Fr. *bocher,* a slaughterer of he-goats. From O. Fr. *boc,* a goat, not from *bouche,* mouth. *Boc* is allied to the Eng. *buck.*

Butler = bottler—that is, keeper of the *bottles.* From Nor. Fr. *butuille,* a bottle.

Buxom, pliable; from *bugan,* to bend, which gives *bight* and *bout.*

Carouse, Ger. *gar aus,* right out. Used of drinking a bumper.

Caterpillar = hairy cat. From O. Fr. *chate,* she-cat; *pelouse,* from Lat. *pilosus,* hairy. Compare *Woolly-bear.*

Causeway, corrupted from Fr. *chaussée,* a raised way.

Club, a society *clumped* together. Connected with *clump*.

Constable, from *comes stabuli*, count of the stable.

Coop, anything hollow, like a *cup*.

Cope, a covering, a *cap*.

Costermonger = costard-monger—that is, apple-seller, costard being a kind of apple.

Country-dance, a corruption of French *contre-danse*, a dance in which each dancer stands *opposite* his partner.

Coward, a bob-*tailed* hare. Through O. Fr., from Lat. *cauda*, a tail.

Coxcomb, a corruption of *cock's comb*.

Daisy—that is, *day's-eye*, so called from its sun-like appearance, or because it closes its flower at night, and opens it again in the morning.

Dandelion, a corruption of French *dent-de-lion*, tooth of the lion.

Dirge, from *dirige* (= *direct*), the first word in the passage beginning Ps. v. 8, sung in the office for the dead.

Disease, want of *ease*; pain.

Drawing-room; originally *with-drawing* room—that is, a room for retiring to after dinner.

Easel, from Dutch *ezel*, a little ass.

Etiquette, originally a *ticket* on which the forms to be observed on particular occasions at court were inscribed.

Fare, originally a *going* or *travelling*, hence the price paid for such.

Farthing, the *fourth* part, hence the fourth of a penny.

Ferry, } places for *faring*, or travelling across a stream.
Ford, }

Frontispiece, that which is seen in the front. Low Lat. *frontispicium*, from *specio*, I see. Not connected with *piece*.

Gad-fly, the *goading* or stinging fly.

Gaffer = *gramfer*, West of England for *grandfather*.

Gammer = *grammer*, West of England for *grandmother*. Compare O. E. *gomman* and *gommer*, for *good man* and *good mother*.

Gospel, *God-spell* (news of God, that is, life of Christ); commonly explained, however, as *good-spell* (good story), as if a translation of Gr. *eu-anggelion*, from *eu*, well, and *anggelia*, a message.

Grocer, should be *grosser*, from O. Fr. *grossier*, a wholesale dealer, a dealer *en gros*—that is, in the large. In older Eng., *grocers* were called *spicers*. Compare the Fr. *épiciers*.

Groove, something *graven*, or hollowed out.

Haft, the handle or part of anything which we *have* or hold in the hand.

Hamper, Low Lat. *hanaperium*, a large vessel for keeping cups, from Low Lat. *hanapus*, a drinking-cup.

Handicraft, *craft* or trade performed by the *hand*. Compare *priest-craft, witchcraft*.

D

Handle, (*v.*) to touch with the *hand*; (*n.*) the part held in the *hand*.

Handsel, money *given* in *hand* (*hand*, and *sellan*, to give).

Hanker, to allow the mind to *hang* on or long for a thing. Compare *hank* of wool.

Harbinger, one who goes forward to provide a harbour or place of *safety* for an *army* (O. E. *here*, an army; *beorgan*, to protect).

Hatch, to produce in a *heck*, a northern English word, meaning a hay-rack; a frame made of cross bars of wood; a hen-coop. Compare *bake* and *batch*; *wake* and *watch*.

Hatchment, the coat of arms put up over a house, the master of which has lately died; a corruption of *achievement*.

Hawthorn, the hedge *thorn*. A.S. *haga*, a hedge or inclosure.

Heaven, that which is *heaved*, or lifted up above our heads.

Heavy, that which requires much *heaving* to lift.

Hinder, to put or keep *behind*.

Homestead, the *stead* or place of a home; a farm inclosure. *Stead*, A.S. *stede*, occurs in in*stead*, *stead*fast, and *stead*y. Cf. also road*stead*, a place where ships ride at anchor.

Husband, the master of a *house*. Short for *house-band*. The *band* is present participle of a word meaning 'to dwell.'

Hussy, short for *housewife*. Compare *bos'n* for *boatswain*.

Icicle = *ice-gicel*. The termination is not to be confounded with the diminutive ending *-icle*, which is of Latin origin. *Gicel* = a small piece of ice, and is therefore redundant.

Intoxicate, to *drug* or poison. From a Low Latin verb to poison, from Greek *toxon*, an arrow, because arrows were frequently dipped in poison.

Island, *water-land* (O. E. *ea*, water, and *land*). The *s* is intrusive, and due to a confusion with *isle*, which is from Lat. *insula*, an island. Milton always spells it *iland*.

Jaw (old spelling, *chaw*), from *chew*, therefore = that which *chews*.

Jerusalem artichoke, It. *girasole*; Lat. *gyrus* (Gr. *gyros*), a circle, and *sol*, the sun. The artichoke is a kind of sunflower. *Jerusalem* is a corruption; like *sparrow-grass* for **asparagus**.

Kickshaws, a corruption of French *quelques choses*.

Kindness, the feeling that is natural to those of the same *kin* or family.

Lanthorn, Lat. *lanterna*. No connection with *horn*.

Ledge, a place on which things may be *laid*. From the verb *lay*.

Likewise, in *like wise* or manner.

Line, to cover with *linen* on the inside.

Linen, cloth made from *lint* or flax.

Liquorice, Gr. *glukurrhiza* = sweet root; from *glukus*, sweet, and *rhiza*, a root.

Meadow, place where grass is *mown* or cut down. Compare *math* and *aftermath*.

Morris-dance = Moorish dance.

Naught, *no-whit*, nothing.

Ness, a promontory or headland. A doublet of *naze*, and probably connected with *nose*. It occurs frequently in place-names along the shores of the North Sea, as in Sheer*ness*, Caith*ness*, the *Naze*.

Nonce, in 'for the nonce' = for the once, for the one occasion ; M. E. *for then ones*. The *n* belongs to the article, and represents the *m* of the dative of the article, namely *tham*. Compare a newt, for an ewt; nuncle for mine uncle ; a nickname for an eke-name ; a nugget or ningot for an ingot.

Nostrils, corrupted form of *nose-thirles*, nose-holes. (Thirl is connected with *thrill, drill*, etc.)

Notwithstanding, *not withstanding*—that is, not standing against. The *with* has in this word the old sense of *against*.

Nurse, one who *nourishes* (Fr. *nourrice*).

Nutmeg = musk-nut. M. E. *note-muge*, O. Fr. *muge*, musk. Lat. *muscus*.

Offal, waste, part of anything, refuse. Literally 'what *falls off*.'

Offing, the sea far *off* from the land. Compare *off-scouring ; offset ; offshoot ;* and *offspring*.

Onset, a *setting* or rushing *on* or upon.

Orchard = *wort-yard*, *wort* or herb-*yard*, or garden.

Ostrich, through O. Fr. *ostruche*, from Lat. *avis struthio*, ostrich bird ; Gr. *struthion*, an ostrich.

Outlaw, one *out* of the protection of the *law*.

Pastime, that which serves to *pass* away the *time*.

Pea-jacket, Dutch *pije*, a rough woollen coat. 'Jacket' is redundant. Not connected with *pea*.

Peal of bells, Fr. *appel*, a call with drum or trumpet.

Penthouse, O. E. *pentice*, Fr. *appentis*, Lat. *appendicium*. Not connected with *house*. A corruption like *Bird-cage Walk* for *Bocage*, (shrubbery) walk.

Pickaxe, O. Fr. *pikois*. No connection with *axe*.

Poach, originally to put into the *pouch* or *pocket*. Cf. to *bag*, to *pocket, sack* and *satchel*.

Pocket, a little *poke* or *pouch*.

Porpoise, the *hog fish*, from Lat. *porcus*, a pig, and *piscis*, a fish.

Proxy, contracted from an obsolete *procuracy*, a taking care of for another.

Quicklime, *lime* in a *quick* or active state. Compare the phrase, 'the quick and the dead.' Cf. also *quick*sand = sand easily moved, *quick*silver, a fluid metal which is very mobile.

Rhyme, properly *rime* = number, confused with rhythm = flow.

Rubbish, that which is *rubbed* off; waste matter.

Scent (for sent), from Lat. *sentio*, I feel.

Sexton, Fr. *sacristain*, sacristan.

Shamefaced, is shame*fast*—that is, shame*fixed*.

Sheaf, a quantity of things, especially the stalks of grain, *shoved* together and bound.

Sheriff, a *shire-reeve*, the *governor* of a *shire* or county.

Ship, something *scooped* or dug out, and therefore hollow. Compare *skipper*, where the hard *k* reappears.

Somerset, a corruption of O. Fr. *soubresault*, from Lat. *supra* and *saltus*, a leaping over.

Sorry, *sore* in mind.

Soup, that which is *supped*.

Splice, to *split* in order to join.

Squirrel, Fr. *écureuil*, Gr. *skiouros* = bushy or shadow tail. From Gr. *skia*, shade, and *oura*, a tail.

Starboard, the *steering* side of a ship—that is, the right hand side to one looking toward the bow.

Stew, to put into a *stove* to be cooked.

Stirrup, put for *sty-rope;* A.S. *stig-rap*, a mounting rope. From the same root are *stair, sty, stile,* and *stag*.

Straight, *stretched* out, tight.

Strong, with the muscles *strung up*. Compare *wrong* from *wring*.

Sweetheart, from *sweet* and *heart*, an expression as old as Chaucer.

Tackle, things to be *taken* hold of.

Tale, that which is told, what is counted. So also *teller* (in a bank).

Thorough, passing *through*, or to the end.

Thread, that which is *thrown* or twisted.

Treacle, Lat. *theriaca*, Gr. *thēriakē*, viper's flesh; *therion* (a wild beast), a name often given to the viper. Originally an antidote to the viper's bite. Milton speaks of 'the treacle of sound doctrine.'

Twist, to twine or wind *two* threads together. (Compare *twine, twirl, twiddle,* etc.)

Verdigris, Fr. *verd-de-grise*, Lat. *viride æris*, green of brass. Not connected with *grease*.

Walrus = *whale horse*, O. E. *hwæl*, whale; *hors*, horse. The *r* has shifted its place, as in *three, third; turn, trundle,* etc.

Whole, hole, O. E. *hæl*. The *w* is redundant; just as it is in the *pronunciation* of *one*. It does not appear in *heal, health,* etc.

Wiseacre, a corruption of the Ger. *weiss sager*, a wise-sayer or sooth-sayer, or prophet.

4. WORDS THAT HAVE CHANGED THEIR MEANING.

Artillery, great weapons of war ; was once used to include crossbows, bows, etc., before gunpowder was invented. 1 Sam. xx. 40 : 'And Jonathan gave his artillery unto his lad, and said unto him, Go, carry *them* to the city.'

Blackguard, a name originally applied to the lowest kitchen servants from the dirty work they had to do.

Bombast, originally cotton-wadding, affected language.

Boor, originally a peasant or tiller of the soil. In South Africa a farmer is called a *boer*.

Brat meant originally a rag or clout, especially a child's bib or apron ; hence, in contempt, a child. Mandeville speaks of 'Abraham's brats.'

Carriage once meant baggage. Acts, xxi. 15 : 'And after those days we took up our carriages, and went up to Jerusalem.'

Censure once meant opinion or judgment. Shakspeare, *As You Like It*, IV. i. 7 : 'Betray themselves to every modern censure.'

Charity, once love, now almsgiving. 1 Cor. xiii. 3 : 'And though I bestow all my goods to feed *the poor*, and though I give my body to be burned, and have not *charity*, it profiteth me nothing.'

Cheat originally meant to seize upon anything which was *escheated* or forfeited.

Churl, a countryman or farmer.

Conceit, originally a thought or notion. 'Dan Chaucer was a conceited clerk'—that is, a learned man full of new inventions or thoughts (conceits).

Cunning, originally knowing, clever, skilled in a craft or trade. The Bible speaks of 'cunning workmen.'

Demure, originally of good manners, now staid, grave.

Disaster, an unkindly *star* (Gr. *astēr*, a star) ; a term from the old astrology.

Fond once meant foolish.

Gazette, a small newspaper, originally a small coin. The newspaper was so named because a *gazetta* was paid for it.

Gossip (*sib*, or related, in *God*), originally a sponsor in baptism. *Gossip* is the kind of talk that goes on between people who are connected with a family. Compare Fr. *commère* and *commèrage*.

Heathen, an unbeliever, originally a dweller on a heath. Compare *pagan*, a dweller in a *pagus*, or country canton.

Idiot, from Gr. *idiōtēs*, a private person. It afterwards meant a person who kept himself aloof from public business and politics ; a person despised by the Athenians.

Imp, formerly used in a good sense, meaning scion or offspring. Now a demon of mischief.

Impertinent, not relating or belonging to the matter in hand.

Influence, a *flowing down* from the stars ; originally a term in astrology.

Kind, originally *born ;* hence *natural*, and so loving.

Knave, originally a boy or servant. Sir John Mandeville speaks of Mohammed as a 'poure knave.'

Miser sometimes means merely a wretched creature. Spenser, *Faerie Queene*, II. i. 8 :
'Vouchsafe to stay your steed for humble miser's sake.'

Officious, sometimes used in a good sense, obliging, serviceable. Shakspeare, *Tit. And.* V. ii. 202:
'Come, come, be every one officious To make this banquet.'

Ostler = hosteller, properly the keeper

of a hostelry or hotel ; now applied to the horse-groom.

Pagan, from *paganus,* a dweller in a canton, a countryman or villager ; hence a heathen or unbeliever. Christianity was first preached in the large cities.

Painful, · originally painstaking. 'Rev. J. Flavel was a painful preacher.'

Polite, from Lat. *politus,* polished.

Prevent (to), originally to go before (*præ* and *venio*). 'Prevent us, O Lord, in all our goings.'

Silly, the *adj.* originally happy, blessed ; whence it came to mean innocent, simple, foolish.

Sycophant (Gr.), originally a *fig-shower ;* a person who informed the police regarding the smuggling of figs into Athens.

Tawdry was applied originally to goods bought at St Audrey's fair (St Audrey = St Ethelreda).

Varlet once meant a serving-man. Valet is a doublet of *varlet.* (From *vassaletus,* an inferior vassal.)

Villain, a farm-servant, a peasant ; from Lat. *villanus,* a servant on a *villa* or farm.

5. WORDS DERIVED FROM THE NAMES OF PERSONS.

Amazon, the name of a nation of war-like women, who were said to cut off their right breasts that they might use the bow. (From Gr. *a,* without, and *mazos,* the breast.)

Argosy, from *Argo,* the name of a famous ship in which the Greek warrior Jason sailed to seek the golden fleece, which was at Colchis, on the eastern shore of the Black Sea.

August was named so in honour of the Roman Emperor Augustus (Cæsar).

Brougham, after Lord Brougham, a famous English lawyer and politician.

Cravat, named from the Croats (Crabats), the people of Croatia, in Austria, from whom we derived the custom of wearing cravats.

Dahlia, from Dahl, a Swede, who introduced the flower into Europe.

Dunce, from Duns Scotus (d. 1308), the great schoolman whose name was used as a term of reproach by his opponents, the followers of the learned Thomas Aquinas.

Filbert, from St. Philibert, whose anniversary falls in the nutting season.

Friday, from Freya, the wife of Odin ; one of the Saxon goddesses.

Galvanism, from Galvani of Bologna, who discovered it. He died in 1798.

Herculean, very powerful ; from Hercules, one of the Greek demi-gods, who was very strong.

Jacobite, one of those who were favourable to the Stuarts ; from Jacobus II., the Latin name for James II.

January, from Janus, the god with two heads, who opened the year.

Jeremiad, a sorrowful story ; from Jeremiah, who wrote the *Lamentations.*

Jovial, cheerful ; from Jove, the king of the ancient gods.

July, from Julius Cæsar, the great Roman statesman and general.

Macadamise, to pave a road with small cubical stones ; from Macadam, who invented this method of making roads. He died 1836.

March, } from Mars, the Roman god
Martial, } of war.

Mausoleum, a magnificent tomb ; from Mausolus, a king of Caria, in Asia Minor, whose widow erected a splendid tomb to his memory.

Mercury, quicksilver ; from Mercury, the light-footed messenger of the gods who dwelt on Olympus.

Panic, from Pan, the god of shepherds, who often appeared to them suddenly and terrified them.

Petrel, a sea-bird; from Peter, who is said to have walked upon the waters.

Philippic, a speech full of strongly passionate language; from Philip, king of Macedon, against whom Demosthenes delivered some fiery speeches of this kind.

Saturday, from Sæter, one of the old Saxon gods.

Saturnine, grave, severe; from Saturn, the father of the Roman gods.

Stentorian, very loud; from Stentor, the name of a Greek herald, who is mentioned by Homer, and who had a very loud voice.

Tantalise, from Tantalus, who is said to have been always thirsty and up to his chin in water, which went out of his reach whenever he tried to drink.

Thursday, from Thor, the Saxon god of thunder.

Tuesday, from Tiew, the Saxon god of war.

Wednesday, the day of Woden or Odin, the Saxon god of war. The *es* is the old possessive form.

6. WORDS DERIVED FROM NAMES OF PLACES.

Academy, a school; from Academia, the name of the gymnasium where Plato, the Greek philosopher, taught his pupils.

Attic, an upper room; from Gr. *Attikos*, Athenian. In Athens the houses are said to have been built with a low upper story.

Bayonet, a kind of dagger, from Bayonne, in France.

Bedlam, a lunatic asylum; from Bethlehem, a monastery in London, which was afterwards used as a madhouse.

Calico, a kind of cotton cloth; from Calicut, in India.

Cambric, fine linen; from Cambray, in French Flanders.

Canary, a bird, and a kind of wine; from Canary Islands, whence these things were brought.

Canter, from Canterbury. The pilgrims to this shrine are said to have ridden at an easy pace.

Cashmere, Cassimere, or Kerseymere, a rich kind of woollen cloth; from Cashmere, a province among the Himalayas, in the north of India, noted for the manufacture of fine woollen fabrics.

Cherry, from Cerāsus, on the Black Sea, whence the fruit was introduced into Europe.

Copper, a metal; from Cyprus, an island in the eastern part of the Mediterranean.

Currant, from Corinth, in Greece, where these small dried grapes were first produced.

Damson, Damask, from Damascus, in Syria.

Dollar, from St Joachim's Thal or valley, in Bohemia. These coins were first made there about 1518, and were called *thalers* or *talers:* whence *dollars.*

Florin, a coin; from Florence, in Italy.

Gin, an alcoholic liquor; from Geneva, in Switzerland. (**Gin**, a trap, is an abbreviation of *engine*.)

Guinea, a coin worth twenty-one shillings; from Guinea (or Gold Coast) in Africa, whence the gold of which these coins were first made was brought.

Gypsy, from Egypt, whence these people were supposed to have come. They really came from India.

Holland, a kind of linen cloth; Hollands, a kind of gin; from Holland.

Indigo, from India.

Jersey, a woollen jacket; from Jersey, one of the Channel Islands.

Magnesia, Magnet, from Magnesia, a town in Asia Minor.

Mantua, a lady's gown; from Mantua, in Italy.

Meander, to wind about; from Mæander, a river in Asia Minor, which had a very winding course.

Milliner, from Milan, in Italy.

Morocco, leather prepared in a certain way; from Morocco, in North Africa.

Nankeen, a kind of cotton cloth; from Nankin, in China.

Port, a dark red wine; from Oporto, in Portugal, whence great quantities of it are shipped.

Sherry, a light-coloured wine; from Xeres, in Spain.

Spaniel, a kind of dog; from Spain.

Turkey, a large domestic fowl; from Turkey, whence the bird was supposed to have come.

Worsted, woollen yarn; from Worsted, the name of a village near Norwich.

7. ENGLISH (OR TEUTONIC) ROOTS.

Ac, an oak; acorn, Acton [oak-town], Uckfield.

Æcer, a field; acre, God's acre [the churchyard].

Æsc, an ash; ash, Ascot, Ashby.

Æthele, noble; Atheling, Ethelbert, Ethelrede [noble in *rede* or counsel].

Bacan, to bake; bake, baker, baxter [a woman baker], batch.

Bana, a slayer; bane, henbane, baneful.

Beám, a tree, or anything in a straight line; beam, sunbeam.

Beorgan, to save or shelter; bury, burgh, harbour, harbinger.

Bígan or beogan, to bend; bow, elbow, buxom.

Bindan, to bind; bind, band, bundle, bond, bandage.

Blówan, to blossom; blow, bloom.

Brecan, to break; break, breakers, breakfast.

Cáld or ceald, cold; cold, chill.

Ceápian, to buy; chapman, Cheapside, cheap, Chippenham, Copenhagen [= Merchants' Haven].

Cunnan, to know, to be able; can, con, cunning.

Cwellan, to slay; quell.

Cwic, alive; quick, quicksand.

Cyning, a king; king, Kingston.

Dragan, to drag; drag, draw, dray, draught, dredge, draggle.

Drypan, to drop; drop, drip, dribble.

Eáge, an eye; eye, eyebright, daisy [= day's eye].

Erian, to plough; ear.

Faran, to go; fare, ferry, wayfarer, fieldfare, ford.

Fleógan, to flee; flee, fly, flight, fledge.

Fleótan, to float; float, fleet.

Fod, food; feed, fodder, foster [= foodster].

Gangan, to go; go, gang, gait, gangway.

Geard, an inclosure; yard, orchard, vineyard.

Gód, good; good, goodwife.

Grafan, to dig; grave, engraver, groove, grove.

Hál, sound; hale, heal, healthy, whole, wholesome.

Healdan, to hold; hold, holding, behold.

Here, an army; harbour, herring, harbinger [a person sent on before to provide quarters for a *here* or army].

Hláf, a loaf; lady, lord, Lammas (loaf-mass).

Hús, a house; house, housewife.

Lædan, to lead; loadstone, loadstar.

Læt, late; late, latter, last, later, belate.

Lang, long; long, length, along, linger.

Lif, life; life, alive.

Mere, a lake; mere, Windermere, marsh.

Móna, the moon; moon, month.

Nosu, or **nasu**, a nose ; nose, the Naze, Ness, nostril, Sheerness.

Rædan, to read ; read, rede, riddle.

Reáfian, to rob ; rob, bereave, rover.

Scíran, to cut; shear, share, shire, shore, short, skirt, ploughshare.

Settan, to place ; **sittan**, to sit ; sit, set, seat, settle.

Spell, a message ; gospel [= good spell].

Stede, a place ; homestead, bedstead.

Stelan, to steal ; steal, stealth.

Stow, a place ; Chepstow, bestow.

Tellan, to reckon ; tell, tale, tell-tale.

Thyrel, a hole ; thrill, nostril, drill.

Tredan, to tread ; tread, treadle.

Wácian, to watch ; wake, watch.

Ward, a looker at or guard ; ward, warden, weir.

Witan, to know ; wit, witness, wisdom, wistful.

Wyrcan, to work ; work, wright.

Wyrt, an herb ; wort, wart, orchard [wort-yard].

8. LATIN ROOTS.

Acer, sharp ; acrid, acrimony, vinegar [= sharp wine].

Acidus, sour ; acid, acidity.

Ædes, a house ; edifice, edify.

Æquus, equal ; equality, equator, adequate, iniquity, equanimity.

Æstimo, I value ; estimation, estimate, esteem.

Ager, a field ; agriculture, peregrinate.

Agger, a heap ; exaggerate.

Ago, I do ; act, agile, agency, cogent.

Alacer, cheerful ; alacrity.

Alo, I nourish ; aliment, alimony.

Alter, the other of two ; alternation, subaltern.

Altus, high ; altitude, exalt.

Ambulo, I walk ; amble, perambulator.

Amo, I love ; amity, amorous, inimical.

Anima, the soul ; animation, inanimate.

Animus, the mind ; magnanimity.

Annus, a circle or year ; annual, perennial.

Aperio, I open ; aperient, April [the opening month, the month of spring when the buds open out].

Appello, I call ; appeal, appellation.

Aptus, fit ; apt, aptitude.

Aqua, water ; aqueduct, aquatic, aqueous.

Arbiter, a judge ; arbitration, arbitrary.

Arbor, a tree ; arboraceous, arbour.

Ardeo, I burn ; ardent, arson.

Arduus, steep [with the idea of difficulty of attainment] ; arduous.

Arma, weapons ; arms, armistice, disarm, army.

Aro, I plough ; arable.

Ars (art-is), art ; artificial, inertia, artisan.

Artus, a joint ; articulate, article.

Audio, I hear ; audience, audible.

Augeo, I increase ; augment, auctioneer.

Avis, a bird ; aviary.

Barba, a beard ; barber, barbel, barb.

Bellum, war ; bellicose, belligerent, rebellious.

Bibo, I drink ; imbibe, winebibber.

Bis, twice ; biscuit, bissextile.

Bonus, good ; benevolent, bounty.

Brevis, short ; brevity, abbreviate, brief.

Cado (cas-um), I fall ; casual, accident.

Cædo (cæs-um), I cut or kill ; precise, excision, decide.

Campus, a plain ; camp, encamp.

Candeo, I shine ; candidus, white, incandescent, candidate.

Cano, I sing ; canticle, chant, incantation.

Capio (capt-um), I take ; captive, accept, reception.

Caput, the head ; capital, captain.

Caro (carn-is), flesh ; carnal, carnival, carnivorous.

Castus, pure ; chastity, castigate, chastise.

Causa, a cause ; accuse, causation.

Caveo (caut-um), I take care ; caution, cautious.

Cavus, hollow ; cavity, cave, excavate.

Cedo (cess-um), I yield ; cede, accede, proceed. I go ; procession, ancestor.

Centum, a hundred; century, centurion.

Cerno (cret-um), I notice or discern ; discern, decretal, discretion.

Cingo (cinct-um), I gird ; cincture, succinct.

Cito, I rouse ; excite, citation.

Civis, a citizen ; civic, civil, city.

Clamo, I shout ; clamour, proclamation, reclaim.

Clarus, clear ; clarify, declare, clarion.

Claudo (claus-um), I shut ; close, exclude, seclusion.

Clivus, a slope ; declivity.

Colo (cult-um), I till ; cultivate, arboriculture.

Copia, plenty ; copious, cornucopia.

Coquo (coct-um), I boil ; decoction, biscuit.

Cor (cord-is), the heart ; courage, cordial, discord.

Corpus (corpor-is), the body ; corpse, corps, incorporate.

Credo, I believe ; credibility, credence, miscreant.

Creo, I create ; create, creation, creature, recreation.

Cresco (cret-um), I grow ; crescent, increment.

Crimen, a charge ; crime, criminate.

Crux (cruc-is), a cross ; crucial, crucifix.

Cubo, I lie down ; incubate, recumbent.

Culpa, a fault ; culpable, exculpate, culprit.

Cura, care ; sinecure, curate, secure, accurate.

Curro (curs-um), I run ; cursory, course, recur, occur.

Decem, ten ; decimal, December.

Dens (dent-is), a tooth ; dentist, dental, indent.

Deus, a god ; deity, deify, divine.

Dexter, right hand ; dexterous.

Dico (dict-um), I say ; verdict, dictation, dictionary, indictment.

Dies, a day ; diary, meridian.

Dignus, worthy ; dignity, indignant.

Do (dat-um), I give ; donor, add [= ad-do, I give to], data.

Doceo (doct-um), I teach ; docile, doctor.

Dominus, a lord ; dominant, dominion, dame.

Domus, a house ; domicile, domestic.

Dormio, I sleep ; dormitory, dormant.

Duco (duct-um), I lead ; induct, education, duke, produce.

Duo, two ; dual, duel, (double), duplex.

Durus, hard ; durable, obdurate, duration.

Emo (empt-um), I buy ; redeem, exemption.

Eo (it-um), I go ; exit, transit, circuit, ambition.

Equus, a horse ; equine, equestrian.

Erro, I wander ; error, aberration.

Esse, to be ; essential, essence.

Facies, the face ; facial, facet, superficial.

Facilis, easy ; facile, facility, difficult.

Facio (fact-um), I make ; manufacture, factor, faction.

Fallo (fals-um), I deceive ; false, infallible, fallacious.

Fama, a report ; fame, defame, infamy.

Fans (fant-is), speaking ; infant [= a non-speaker].

Felix (felic-is), happy ; felicity, infelicity.

Fero, I bear or carry ; infer, reference, difference.

Ferrum, iron ; ferruginous.

Ferveo, I boil ; fervent, effervesce, ferment.

Fido, I trust ; confide, infidel, perfidy, diffident.

Filius, a son ; filial, affiliation.

Filum, a thread ; file, defile, profile.

Finis, an end ; final, infinite, confine.

Firmus, firm ; infirm, affirm.

Flecto, I bend ; flexible, inflection.

Flos (flōr-is), a flower ; floral, Flora, floriculture.

Fluo (fluct-um), I flow ; fluent, flux, refluent, fluid.

Forma, a form ; form, formal, reform, conformity.

Fortis, strong ; fortify, fortitude, fortress.

Frango (fract-um), I break ; fragile, fragmentary, infraction.

Frater, a brother ; fraternal, fratricide.

Frons (front-is), the forehead ; frontispiece, frontal, frontier.

Fruor (fruct-us), I enjoy ; fruit, fructify, fruition.

Fugio, I flee ; fugitive, refugee, subterfuge.

Fundo (fus-um), I pour ; fusible, diffusion, foundry.

Fundus, the bottom ; foundation, profound.

Furor, madness ; furious, fury.

Gelu, frost ; gelid, jelly, congeal.

Gens (gent-is), a nation ; gentile, genteel, gentle, congenial.

Genus (genĕr-is), a kind ; general, genus.

Gero (gest-um), I bear or carry ; gesture, suggestion.

Gradior (gress-us), I go ; gradus, a step ; degrade, progress, degree.

Grandis, great ; grand, aggrandise.

Gratia, favour ; gratiæ, thanks ; gratitude, ingratiate, gratis.

Gravis, heavy ; gravitate, gravity, (grief).

Grex (greg-is), a flock ; gregarious, egregious.

Habeo, I have ; habit, able, exhibit, prohibition.

Hæreo (hæs-um), I stick ; adhere, cohesion.

Homo, a man ; homicide, human.

Hospes (hospit-is), a guest ; hospital, hostel, hotel.

Hostis, an enemy ; host, hostile.

Humus, the ground ; posthumous, exhume.

Ignis, fire ; ignite, igneous.

Impero, I command ; imperial, emperor, empire.

Insula, an island ; isle, insular, peninsula, insulate. [*Island* is not connected with this root. It was in older English spelled *iland*.]

Iter (itiner-is), a journey ; itinerant.

Jacio (jact-um), I throw ; adjective, project, injection.

Judex (judic-is) ; (adjudge), judicial.

Jungo (junct-um), I join ; junction, conjoin, juncture.

Jus (jur-is), law, right ; justice, jurisdiction, jury.

Labor (laps-us), I glide ; lapse, collapse.

Lædo (læs-um), I injure ; collision, lesion.

Lapis (lapīd-is), a stone ; lapidary.

Latus, broad ; latitude.

Laus (laud-is), praise ; laud, laudable.

Lego (lect-um), I gather or read ; college, collect, prelection, lecture.

Lēvis, light ; levity, alleviate, relief.

Lex (lēg-is), law ; legal, legislate.

Liber, free ; liberal, liberty.

Libra, a balance ; deliberate.

Ligo, I bind ; ligament, religion.

Limes (limit-is), a boundary ; limit.

Linquo (lict-um), I leave ; relinquish, relict, relics.

Litera, a letter ; literature, literary, letters, obliterate.

Locus, a place ; location, dislocate.

Longus, long ; elongate, longitude.

Loquor (locūt-us), I speak ; loquacious, eloquent, elocution.

Ludo (lus-um), I play ; ludicrous, allusion.

Lumen (lumin-is), light ; illuminate, luminous.

Luna, the moon ; Luna, sublunary, lunacy.

Luo, I wash ; ablution, dilute.

Lux (luc-is), light ; lucid, pellucid.

Magister, a master ; magistrate, master.

Magnus, great ; magnificent, magniloquent, magnify.

Malus, bad; malady, malice, maltreat.

Maneo (mans-um), I remain; mansion, permanent.

Manus, the hand; manufacture, manual, manuscript.

Mare, the sea; marine, mariner.

Mater, a mother; maternal, matricide.

Maturus, ripe; mature, maturity.

Medeor, I heal; medicine, remedy.

Medius, the middle; medial, immediate, Mediterranean.

Memini, I remember; **memor,** mindful; memorable, commemorate, memento, immemorial.

Mens (ment-is), the mind; mental, comment.

Mereo (merit-um), I deserve; merit, meretricious.

Mergo (mers-um), I dip; submerge, immersion.

Merx (merc-is), goods; merchant, commerce, mercantile.

Miles (milit-is), a soldier; military, militant, militia.

Mille, a thousand; mile, million.

Miror, I admire; admire, miracle, mirage.

Misceo, I mix; miscellaneous, promiscuous.

Mitto (miss-um), I send; mission, missile, remittance.

Modus, a measure; modify, mood, accommodate.

Mollis, soft; mollify, emollient.

Moneo (monit-um), I advise; admonition, monitor.

Mons (mont-is), a mountain; mountain, promontory.

Monstro, I point out; demonstrate.

Mors (mort-is), death; mortify, mortal.

Moveo (mot-um), I move; motion, movable, move.

Multus, many; multiplex, multitude.

Munus (muner-is), a gift; remunerate, munificent.

Muto, I change; mutable, immutable, transmute.

Nascor (nat-us), to be born; nascent, natal, nativity.

Navis, a ship; navigate, naval, navy.

Necto (nex-us), I tie; connect, nexus, annex.

Nego, I deny; negative, negation.

Noceo, I hurt; noxious, innocuous, innocent.

Nomen (nomin-is), a name; nominal, nomination, cognomen.

Nosco (not-um), I know or mark; note, notation.

Novus, new; novel, novitiate, innovation.

Nox (noct-is), night; nocturnal, equinoctial.

Nudus, naked; nude, denudation.

Numero, I number; enumerate, numeration.

Nuntio, I announce; nuncio, annunciation, pronounce.

Nutrio, I nourish; nutriment, nurse.

Octo, eight; octave, octagon, October.

Oculus, the eye; oculist.

Odor, smell; odour, redolent.

Omnis, all; omnipotent, omniscient.

Onus (oner-is), a burden; onerous.

Opus (oper-is), a work; operate, operation.

Ordo (ordin-is), order; ordinal, ordinary.

Oro, I pray; oration, inexorable, peroration.

Os (or-is), the mouth; oral, adore.

Os (oss-is), bone; ossify, ossification.

Pando (pans-um or pass-um), I spread; expand, expanse, compass.

Pango (pact-um), I fix; compact, impinge.

Panis, bread; pantry, pannier, company.

Par, equal; (pair), par, parity.

Pareo, I appear; apparent, apparition.

Paro (parat-um), I prepare; prepare, repair, apparatus.

Pars (part-is), a part; partition, particle.

Pasco (past-um), I feed; repast, pastor.

Pater, a father; paternal, patricide.

Patior (pass-us), I suffer; impatient, passion.

Pauper, poor; pauper, poverty.

Pax (pāc-is), peace; pacify, pacific.

Pello (puls-um), I drive; repel, expel, expulsion.

Pendeo (pens-um), I hang; dependent, suspend.

Pendo, I weigh out, hence, I pay; expend, recompense.

Pes (pĕd-is), the foot; impede, pedestrian, biped.

Peto (petit-um), I seek; petition, petulant.

Pingo (pict-um), I paint; picture, pigment.

Placeo, I please; placid, complacent.

Planus, level; plane, plain, plan.

Plaudo (plaus-um), I clap the hands; applause, (explode).

Plecto (plex-um), I weave; complex, perplex.

Pleo (plĕt-um), I fill; complete, completion, repletion.

Plico, I fold; complicate, reply.

Plus (plūr-is), more; plurality, surplus.

Pœna, punishment; penalty, repent.

Pondus (pondĕr-is), weight; ponderous, pound.

Pono (posĭt-um), I place; disposition, exposition, imposition.

Pons (pont-is), a bridge; pontiff, transpontine.

Popŭlus, the people; populace, popular.

Porto, I carry; export, deportation, report.

Possum, I am able; potens, able; possible, potency, potentate, impotent.

Poto, I drink; potion, poison, potable.

Precor, I pray; precarious, imprecation.

Prehendo, I take; apprehend, comprehension, apprentice.

Premo (press-um), I press; compress, print.

Pretium, a price; precious, appreciate, prize.

Primus, first; prime, primitive, primrose.

Privo, I separate; deprive, privateer, private.

Probo, I try or prove; probable, prove, reproof.

Proprius, one's own; property, appropriation.

Pugna, a fight; pugnacious, repugnant.

Pungo (punct-um), I prick; pungent, poignant, punctual.

Puto, I cut or think; amputate, compute, reputation.

Quæro (quæsit-um), I seek; quest, inquiry, inquisition.

Quatuor, four; quadrilateral, square, quarry, quart, quadrant.

Quies (quiĕt-is), rest; acquiesce, quiet, requite.

Radius, a ray; radiant, irradiate, (ray).

Radix (radic-is), a root; radical, eradicate.

Rapio (rapt-um), I seize; rapture, rapine, surreptitious.

Ratio, reason; rational, ration, reason.

Rego (rect-um), I rule; regiment, regal, regulate, rector, rectify.

Res (re-i), a thing; real, reality, republican.

Rex (reg-is), a king; regal, interregnum, royal.

Rideo (rīs-um), I laugh; deride, derision.

Rivus, a brook; river, rival.

Rodo (ros-um), I gnaw; erosion, corrode.

Rogo, I ask; derogatory, interrogation, arrogate.

Rota, a wheel; rote, rotation, rotund, round.

Rumpo (rupt-um), I break; rupture, disruption, irruption, eruption.

Rus (rūr-is), the country; rural, rustic.

Sacer, sacred; desecrate, sacrilege.

Sal, salt; saline, salary [=salt-money].

Salio (salt-um), I leap; (sally, assail, assault, insult, salmon [= the *leaping* fish], salient.

Salus (salūt-is), health ; salvus, safe; salutary, salubrious, salvation.

Sanctus, holy ; sanctify, saint.

Sanguis (sanguin-is), blood ; sanguinary.

Sano (sanāt-um), I cure ; sanitary, sane, insane.

Sapio, I taste or am wise ; sapient, insipid, savour.

Scando (scans-um), I climb; scala, a ladder; scan, scale, ascension, descend.

Scio, I know ; science, scientific, conscience, omniscient.

Scribo (script-um), I write; scribe, scripture, manuscript, describe.

Seco (sect-um), I cut ; dissect, insect, segment, section.

Sedeo (sess-um), I set; sediment, subside, residence.

Senex, an old man ; senile, senior, senate, senator.

Sentio (sens-us), I feel or perceive ; sense, sentimental.

Septem, seven ; septennial, September.

Sequor (secūt-us), I follow; sequel, consecutive, consequent.

Servio, I serve ; servant, service, servitor.

Servo, I preserve ; reserve, conservative, conservatory.

Signum, a mark ; sign, signify, designation.

Similis, like ; dissimilar, similitude, resemble, dissemble.

Sisto, I stop ; insist, consistency.

Solus, alone ; solitary, sole.

Solvo (solūt-um), I loose ; absolute, resolve, solution, resolution.

Somnus, sleep ; somnolent, somnambulist.

Specio (spect-um) I see ; aspect, retrospect, specions.

Spero, I hope ; despair, desperate.

Spiro, I breathe ; spiral, aspire, inspiration, conspiracy.

Spondeo (spons-um), I promise; respond, sponsor, (spouse).

Statuo, I set up ; sto (stat-um), to stand ; statute, statue, institute, restitution, extant, substance.

Stella, a star ; stellar, constellation.

Stringo (strict-um), I bind ; stringent, stricture, constrain.

Struo (struct-um), I build ; structure, (construe, destroy), destruction.

Suadeo (suas-um), I persuade ; persuasion, dissuade.

Sumo (sumpt-um), I take; resume, consumption.

Surgo (surrect-um), I arise ; insurgent, resurrection.

Taceo, I am silent ; tacit, taciturn.

Tango (tact-um), I touch ; intangible, contact, contagions.

Tego (tect-um), I cover : integument, detect.

Tempus (tempŏr-is), time ; temporal, tense.

Tendo (tens-um), I stretch ; extend, intension, tent, tense.

Teneo (tent-um), I hold ; contain, tenacious, retentive.

Terminus, an end or boundary ; term, terminus, determine.

Tero (trīt-um), I rub ; contrition, trite, detritus.

Terra, the earth ; subterranean, Mediterranean.

Terreo, I frighten ; terror, terrify.

Testis, a witness; testator, testify, contest.

Texo (text-um), I weave ; texture, context, textile.

Timeo, I fear ; timid, intimidation.

Tono, I thunder ; astonish, detonate.

Torqueo (tort-um), I twist; torture, torsion.

Traho (tract-um), I draw ; contractile.

Tribuo, I give ; tribute, contribution.

Tribus, a tribe ; tribe, tribune, tribunal.

Trudo (trus-um), I thrust ; extrusion, intrude.

Turba, a crowd ; turbid, turbulent.

Umbra, a shadow ; umbrage, adumbration.

Unda, a wave ; undulate, inundation.

Unguo (unct-um), I anoint; unguent, unctuous, ointment.
Unus, one; unity, union.
Urbs, a city; urban, suburb.
Utor (us-us), I use; use, utensil, usury.
Vacca, a cow; vaccinate.
Valeo, I am strong; valour, valiant, prevail.
Vanus, empty; vain, vanish, vanity.
Vas (vās-is), a vessel; vase, vascular, vessel.
Veho (vect-um), I carry; vehicle, convey.
Vello (vuls-um), I pluck; convulsion.
Venio (vent-um), I come; venture, advent.
Ver, the spring; verdant, vernal, verdure.
Verbum, a word; verb, verbal, verbose, proverb.
Verto (vers-um), I turn; controvert, aversion.
Verus, true; verdict, veracious, verity.

Vestis, a garment; invest, vesture.
Vetus (vetĕr-is), old; veteran.
Via, a way; deviate, previous.
Video (vis-um), I see; vision, provident.
Vinco (vict-um), I overcome; victor, victory, convince.
Vir, a man; virtue, virile.
Vita, life; vital, vitality.
Vitium, a fault; vitiate, vicious, vice.
Vivo (vict-um), I live; survive, victuals.
Voco, I call; vox (vōc-is), the voice; voice, convocation, revoke, vociferate.
Volo, I fly; volatile, volley.
Volo, I wish; involuntary, volition, benevolence, malevolence.
Volvo (volūt-um), I roll; involution, evolve, volume.
Voveo (vot-um), I vow; vow, devote.
Vulgus, the common people; vulgar, divulge.
Vulnus (vulnĕr-is), a wound; vulnerable.

9. GREEK ROOTS.

Ago, I lead; pedagogue, synagogue.
Agōn, a contest; agony, antagonist.
Allos, another; allopathy, allegory.
Anggelos, a messenger; angel, evangelist.
Anthrōpos, a man; misanthrope, philanthropy.
Archo, I begin or rule; monarch, archaic [= early]; archbishop, archdeacon.
Arctos, a bear; Arctic, Antarctic, Arcturus.
Arithmos, number; arithmetic.
Aster or astron, a star; astronomy, astrology, asteroid, disaster.
Atmos, vapour; atmosphere.
Autos, self; autocrat, autograph.
Ballo, I throw; symbol.
Bapto, I dip; baptise, baptist.
Baros, weight; barometer.
Biblos, a book; Bible, bibliomania.

Bios, life; biography, biology.
Cheir, the hand; surgeon [older form, chirurgeon].
Chrio, I anoint; Christ, chrism.
Cholē, bile; melancholy.
Chronos, time; chronology, chronic, chronicle.
Daktŭlos, a finger; dactyl, pterodactyl, date—the fruit.
Deka, ten; decagon, decalogue.
Dēmos, the people; democrat, endemic, epidemic.
Dokeo, to think; doxa and dogma, an opinion; doxology, orthodox, heterodox, dogma, dogmatic.
Drao, I do; drama, dramatic.
Dunamis, power; dynamics.
Eidos, form; kaleidoscope.
Eikon, an image; iconoclast.
Electron, amber; electricity.
Ergon, a work; surgeon [= chirurgeon], energy.

Eu, well; eucharist, euphony, evangelist.

Gamos, marriage; bigamy, monogamist, misogamy.

Gē, the earth; geography, geometry, geology.

Gennao, I produce; genesis, genealogy, hydrogen, oxygen.

Grapho, I write; gramma, a letter; graphic, grammar, telegraph, biography, diagram.

Haima, blood; hæmorrhage, hæmorrhoid.

Haireo, I take away; heresy, heretic.

Helios, the sun; helioscope, heliotype.

Hemi, half; hemisphere.

Hieros, sacred; hierarchy, hieroglyphic.

Hippos, a horse; hippopotamus, hippodrome.

Hŏdos, a way; method, period, exodus.

Hŏmos, the same; homœopathy, homogeneous.

Hudŏr, water; hydraulic, hydrophobia.

Ichthus, a fish; ichthyology.

Idios, one's own; idiom, idiot, idiosyncrasy.

Isos, equal; isochronous, isobaric (of equal weight).

Kalos, beautiful; caligraphy, calotype.

Kephalē, the head; hydrocephalus.

Klino, I bend; climax, climate.

Kosmos, order; cosmogony, cosmography, cosmetic.

Krino, I judge; critic, criterion, hypocrite.

Kuklos, a circle; cycle, cycloid, cyclone.

Kuon, a dog; cynic, cynicism.

Lego, I say or choose; eclectic, lexicon.

Lithos, a stone; lithograph, aerolite.

Logos, a word, speech; logic, dialogue, geology.

Luo, I loosen; dialysis, analysis.

Metron, a measure; metronome, diameter, thermometer, barometer.

Mŏnos, alone; monastery, monogram, monosyllable.

Morphē, shape; amorphous, dimorphous, metamorphic.

Naus, a ship; nautical.

Nekros, a dead body; necropolis, necromancy.

Nŏmos, a law; autonomous, astronomy, Deuteronomy.

Oikos, a house; economy, economical.

Onŏma, a name; anonymous, synonymous, patronymic.

Optŏmai, I see; optics, synoptical.

Orthos, right; orthodoxy, orthography.

Pais (paid-os), a boy; pedagogue [lit. a boy-leader].

Pan, all; pantheist, panoply, pantomime.

Pathos, feeling; pathetic, sympathy.

Pente, five; pentagon, pentateuch, Pentecost.

Phainŏmai, I appear; phantasy, phantom, fantastic, fancy.

Phero, I bear; periphery, phosphorus [= the light-bearer].

Phileo, I love; philosophy, Philadelphia.

Phōs (phŏt-os), light; photometer, photograph.

Phusis, nature; physics, physiology, physician.

Planao, I cause to wander; planet.

Poieo, I make; poet, poetic, pharmacopœia.

Polis, a city; Constantinople, metropolis.

Polus, many; polytheist, Polynesia, polyanthus.

Pous (pŏd-os), a foot; antipodes.

Pur, fire; pyrotechnic, pyre.

Rheo, I flow; rhetoric, catarrh, rheumatic.

Skŏpeo, I see; microscope, telescope, spectroscope, bishop [from episkopos, an overseer].

Sophia, wisdom; sophist, philosophy.

Stello, I send; apostle, epistle.

Stratos, an army; strategy, strategic.

Strĕpho, I turn ; catastrophe.

Technĕ, an art ; technical.

Tĕlĕ, distant ; telegraph, telescope, telephone, telegram.

Temno, I cut : anatomy, lithotomy.

Tetra, four ; tetrachord, tetrarch.

Theăomai, I see, behold : theatre, theory.

Theos, a god ; theist, enthusiast, theology.

Thermĕ, heat ; thermal, thermometer, isotherm.

Tithĕmi, I place ; thĕsis, a placing ; synthesis, hypothesis.

Treis, three ; triangle, trigonometry, trilobite.

Trĕpo, I turn ; trophy, tropic.

Tupos, the impress of a seal ; type, stereotype.

Zŏon, an animal ; zoology, zodiac.

10. THE BRANCHING OF WORDS FROM LATIN STEMS.

Ag-o (act-um), I do.—Act, that which is done ; active, engaged in doing ; action, a doing ; enact, to make an *act*, to establish as law ; enactment : transaction, the doing of a thing thoroughly ; react, to do again.

Apt-us, fitted.—Apt, fit : aptitude, fitness ; adapt, to fit to ; adaptability, capability of being fitted to ; adaptation, a fitting to ; adept, one who is fitted for doing things.

Ced-o, I go.—Accede, to go to, hence to agree to ; access, a going to, hence an approach or entrance ; accessory, going to or aiding ; concede, to go away from, to give up ; concession, the act of giving up ; exceed, to go out of : excess, that which goes out or beyond ; excessive, going beyond ; intercede, to go in between, hence to act as a peacemaker ; intercessory, going in between ; precede, to go before ; procession, a going forth, or that which goes forth ; recede, to go back : recess, a space which goes back ; succeed, to come from under, hence to follow in order ; success, the act of succeeding ; successor, one who follows ; successively, following in order.

Cor (cord-is), the heart.—Cordial, hearty ; cordiality, heartiness ; concord, state of being of the same heart, harmony ; discord, want of heart or agreement ; discordant ;

record, to call back to the heart or mind ; recorder, one who keeps records or registers ; courage (through Fr.), heart—that is, bravery ; encourage, to put heart in ; discourage, to take heart from ; discouragement.

Cur-a, care.—Cure (verb and noun) ; curable, that may be cured ; cureless, without cure ; curate, one who has the cure (or care) of souls ; curator, one who has care of anything ; curative, tending to cure ; curious, full of care, anxious ; curiosity ; ¡accurate, done with care, hence without error ; procure, to take care of ; procurator, one who takes care of ; secure, free from care ; security, state of being free from care ; sinecure, an office without care.

Curr-o, I run.—Current, that which runs ; currency, a running, the money which runs in a country ; concur, to run together, hence to agree ; incur, to run into ; occur, to run in the way of ; recur, to run back : ·course (through Fr.), the track on which anything runs ; courser, a runner ; recourse, a running back, a going to for aid ; intercourse, a running between ; precursor, one who runs before ; courier (Fr.), one who runs : corridor (Spanish), a passage or gallery running along.

Do (dat-um, what is given), I give.—

E

Add, to give to ; **addition**, act of giving to ; **condition**, state in which things are put together, or exist ; **conditionally** ; **edit**, to give forth or out ; **edition**, what is given out ; **editor**, one who gives out ; **date**, the time given in a letter.

Duc-o, I lead.—**Duke**, a leader ; **ducal**, pertaining to a leader ; **ductile**, that which may be led or drawn out ; **ductility**, the quality of being ductile ; **educate**, to lead out ; **education** ; **conduct** (verb and noun), to lead together ; **induce**, to lead into ; **produce**, to lead forth ; **reduce**, to lead back ; **seduce**, to lead out of the right path.

Dur-us, hard.—**During**, lasting (but now used as a *preposition*) ; **dure**, to last ; **duration** ; **durable** ; **durability** ; **durableness** ; **endure**, to be hard, firm, or lasting ; **obdurate**, hardened against.

Fac-io, I do, or I make.—**Fact**, a deed ; **factor**, a maker ; **affect**, to act upon ; **affection** ; **affected** ; **affectation**, acting upon one's self ; **defect**, a want ; **effect**, something thoroughly done ; **effective** ; **perfect**, to make thoroughly ; **perfection**, state of being thoroughly made ; **imperfect**, not thoroughly made.

Fer-o, I carry.—**Confer**, to come together for council ; **conference** ; **defer**, to bear one's self down or yield to the wishes of another ; **deference** ; **differ**, to carry asunder, hence to disagree ; **different** ; **differently** ; **difference** ; **offer**, to carry in the way of ; **prefer**, to carry before, hence to esteem more than another ; **preference** ; **refer**, to carry back ; **suffer**, to bear up, hence to undergo ; **transfer**, to carry across.

Firm-us, strong.—**Firm**, strong ; **firmness** ; **firmly** ; **confirm**, to make more strong ; **confirmation** ; **affirm**, to declare strongly ; **infirm**, not strong ; **infirmity**, state of being infirm, hence disease ; **infirmary**, a place for the infirm ; **firmament**, that which is firm, the place supposed to be fixed above the earth.

Form-a, shape.—**Form**, shape ; **formal**, according to form ; **informal**, not according to form ; **formality** ; **formally** ; **formative**, giving form ; **formula**, a little form ; **conform**, to make of the same form with ; **deform**, to alter or injure the form of ; **inform**, to put into form or shape, educate, instruct ; **information** ; **misinform**, to give wrong knowledge to ; **perform**, to form thoroughly ; **reform**, to form again ; **reformation** ; **transform**, to change the form of.

Grati-a, favour.—**Grace** (through Fr.) ; **graceful**, full of the power to win favour ; **gracefulness** ; **gracefully** ; **gracious**, full of grace ; **disgrace**, state of being out of grace or favour ; **grateful**, thankful for favour ; **ingratitude** ; **ingrate**, an ungrateful person ; **gratify**, to please ; **gratuitous**, by favour and without price ; **gratitude** ; **agree** (Fr.).

Habe-o, I have.—**Habit**, the having one's self in a certain condition ; **habitual** ; **habitable**, that may be inhabited ; **habitat**, the place which a plant or an animal inhabits ; **habitation**, place where one dwells or inhabits ; **exhibit**, to hold out to view ; **inhibit**, to hold in or keep back ; **inhibition** ; **inhabit**, to be in the habit of living in ; **prohibit**, to hold before one, hence to check.

Jac-io (jact-um), I throw.—**Eject**, to throw out ; **ejectment**, a throwing out ; **ejection**, the act of throwing out ; **ejaculate**, to throw out (a sound) ; **ejaculation** ; **abject**, thrown down ; **adjective**, that which is thrown to or added to ; **conjecture**, a throwing together of chances, or a guess ; **deject**, to throw down ; **inject**, to throw into ; **interjection**, a throwing into the middle of; project (verb and noun), to throw forward; subject (verb and noun), to throw under; reject, to throw back.

Jung-o (junct-us, joined), I join.—Join (through Fr.); joint, a place where things are joined; joiner, one who joins; juncture, a joining; conjoin (Fr.), to join together; conjuncture, a joining together; disjoin (Fr.), to separate; adjunct, something joined to; conjunction, that which joins together.

Leg-o (lect-um), I gather or read.—Collect', to gather together; col'lect, what is gathered together; collection; collector; elect, to gather out from; election; elector; select, to choose apart, to pick out; legend, that which should be read; legible, that which may be read.

Mitt-o (miss-um), I send.—Admit; commit, to send together with, to intrust to; commitment, a sending together; commission, a sending with authority; emit, to send out; emission, a sending out; omit, to send away, to leave out; omission, the act of leaving out; permit; permission; remit, to send back; transmit, to send through.

Norm-a, a rule.—Normal, according to rule; normally; enormous, great, beyond rule; enormity; abnormal, away from rule.

Nosc-o (not-um), I know or mark.—Note, something by which a thing may be known, hence a mark; noted, known; notable, deserving to be known; noble (Fr.); notify, to make known; notorious, too well known; notice, a warning to know; noticeable, likely to be observed or known.

Ord-o (ordin-is), arrangement.—Order; ordain, to arrange or put in order; ordinal, that which shows arrangement; ordination, the act of arranging; ordinary, according to the common arrangement; extra-ordinary, out of the common arrangement; disorder, want of arrangement; orderly, properly arranged.

Pars (part-is), a part.—Part; particle, a small part; tripartite, divided into three parts; partition, that which divides into parts; partial, relating to a part only; apart, parted from; depart, to part from; impart, to give part to.

Pell-o (puls-um), I drive.—Compel, to drive together; compulsion, the act of driving together; dispel, to drive asunder; expel, to drive out; expulsion; impel, to drive forward (or into); impulse; propel, to drive forward; repel, to drive back; repulse.

Pend-o (pens-um), I hang.—Append, to hang to; appendage, something hung on to; depend, to hang down from; dependant, one who hangs from another; independent, not hanging from another; independence, the state of not hanging from another; pendant, that which hangs; suspend, to hang under; suspense, state of hanging [under].

Pon-o (posit-um), I place.—Post, something placed, and hence the place in which it stands; position, state of being placed, hence place; composition, a placing together; opposition, a placing in the way of; proposition, a placing before.

Port-o, I carry.—Porter, one who carries; export, to carry out of a country; import, to carry into a country; report, to carry back, to repeat; report, what is carried back or repeated; reporter; support, to bear up from under; transport, to carry across; transportation.

Prem-o (press-um), I press.—Press; compress, to press together; compression, the act of pressing together; depress, to press down; express, to press out, hence to utter or say; **impress'**, to press into (as of a seal); **im'press**, the mark left by anything impressed; **repress**, to press back; **suppress**, to press under.

Rect-us, right.—**Rectify**, to make right; **rectitude**, state of being right; **correct**, to put right; **cor'rector**; **correction**, a putting right.

Reg-o (rect-um), I rule.—**Regal**, pertaining to a king or ruler; **rector**, one who rules (in the church); **rectory**, the house in which the rector lives.

Rump-o (rupt-um), I break.—**Abrupt**, broken off; **rupture**, a breaking; **corrupt**, to break thoroughly, to break in pieces; **corrupt** (*adj.*) broken in pieces; **corruptible**, that which may be corrupted; **irruption**, a breaking into; **eruption**, a breaking out; **disruption**, a breaking asunder.

Scrib-o (script-um), I write.—**Scribe**, one who writes; **describe**, to write down; **inscribe**, to write upon; **inscription**; **subscribe**, to write under; **subscription**; **scripture**, that which is written.

Sed-eo (sess-um), I sit.—**Sedentary**, in the habit of sitting; **preside**, to sit before others, hence to be in authority; **assiduous**, sitting close to (work); **subside**, to sit under, hence to settle; **session**, a sitting.

Serv-o (servat-um), I keep.—**Conserve**, to keep together; **conservatory**, a place for keeping things together; **observe**, to keep in the way of (the eyes), hence to keep in view; **observatory**, a place for observing (the stars); **reserve**, to keep back; **reserve**, what is kept back.

Spec-io (spect-um), I look.—**Aspect**, look; **spectator**, one who looks at; **speculum**, a looking-glass; **suspicion**, a looking under.

Statu-o (statut-um), I set up.—**Statue**, something set up; **statute**, a law set up.

Tang-o (tact-um), I touch.—**Tangent**, a line which touches; **tangible**, which may be touched; **tactile**, that which can touch; **contact**, touching; **tact**, the art of knowing as it were by mere touch.

Tend-o (tent-um or tens-um), I stretch.—**Distend**, to stretch asunder; **extend**, to stretch out; **extent**, the amount a thing stretches; **tense**, stretched; **tent**, something which is stretched.

Ten-eo (tent-um), I hold.—**Tenant**, one who holds (a house or land); **tenacious**, holding much or firmly; **contain**, to hold together; **detain**, to hold down, hence to hinder; **retain**, to hold back; **retentive**, holding back or keeping.

Trah-o (tract-um), I draw.—**Attract**, to draw to; **contract**, to draw together; **traction**, the act of drawing; **subtract**, to draw from under, hence to take away; **subtrahend**, that which has to be taken away; **contraction**, a drawing together.

Ut-or (us-us), I use.—**Use**; **abuse**, to use away from its proper purpose; **peruse**, to use thoroughly, hence to read through; **usury**, money paid for the use of money; **utensil**, something to be used; **utility**, usefulness.

Veh-o (vect-um), I carry.—**Vehicle**, that in which goods are carried; **convey**, to carry together; **conveyance**, that in which goods are carried together.

Ven-io (vent-um), I come.—**Convene**, *originally* to come together, *afterwards* to summon; **convention**; **advent**, a coming to; **intervene**, to come in between; **contravene**, to come against, hence to oppose; **circumvent**, to come round; **intervention**, the act of coming in between.

Vert-o (vers-um), I turn.—**Convert**, to turn together; **conversion**, the act of turning together; **advert**, to turn towards; **divorce**, to turn asunder; **invert**, to turn into; **inversion**, the act of turning into; **reverse**, to turn back; **verse**, a kind of composition in which the writer *turns back* from the end of the line.

Vid-eo (**vis-um**), I see.—**Visitor**, one who sees; **vision**, what is seen; **visual**, pertaining to seeing; **visible**, what may be seen; **provide**, to see before; **providence**, a seeing before-hand; **prudence** (Fr.), another form of *providence*.

Voc-o (**vocat-um**), I call.—**Convoke**, to call together; **convocation**, a meeting which has been called together; **revoke**, to call back; **vocal**, calling—that is, having a voice; **voice**, that by which one calls; **vociferate**.

Volv-o (**volut-um**), I roll.—**Convolution**, a rolling together; **revolve**, to roll round; **involve**, to roll into.

11. THE BRANCHING OF WORDS FROM ENGLISH STEMS.

Bac-an, to bake.—**Bake**; **baker**; **baxter** (bakester), a woman who bakes; **batch**, what is baked.

Beat-an, to strike.—**Bat**, an instrument to strike a ball with; **beetle**, an instrument to beat clothes with.

Ber-an, to carry.—**Bearer**; **burden**; **barrow**, that on which something is borne; **bier**, that on which a corpse is borne; **forbear**, to bear forth or off, hence to abstain; **overbear**, to bear over, to overpower.

Brec-an, to break.—**Break**, an instrument for breaking the speed of a train; **breach**, a break in a wall; **brook**, a stream which breaks from the ground.

Brinn-an, to burn.—**Burn**; **brown** is the burnt colour; **brand**, a mark made by burning; **brandy**, a drink made by burning wine; **brunt**, the burning or hottest part of a fight; **brimstone**, burning stone (a name for sulphur); **brindled**, striped with brown; **bran new** [= brand new].

Drag-an, to pull.—**Drag**; **draw**, another form of drag; **dray**, a kind of cart which is drawn along; **draught**, what is drawn; **draft**, a cheque drawn on a banker; **drain**, a ditch for drawing off water; **drawl**, to keep drawing out one's words.

Far-an, to go.—**Far**, that which requires much going to reach; **farewell**, go well! **fieldfare**, a bird which goes in the fields; **thoroughfare**, a place where people go through; **ford**, a place in a river where one can go across on foot; **ferry**, a place in a river where one can go over in a boat; **fare**, the money paid for going.

Hæl, sound.—**Hale**; **heal**, to make hale; **health**, state of being sound or hale; **healthy**; **healthful**; **holy**, spiritually hale; **hail**, be hale! or be healthy! **whole**, in a state of being hale (the *w* is intrusive); **wholesome**, what tends to make hale.

Lig, lie.—**Lie**, to lie down; **lay**, to make to lie; **lair**, the place where a wild beast lies; **law**, what lies or is in due order; **low**, what is (lying) down.

Maw-an, to mow.—**Mower**; **math**, the grass that is mowed; **aftermath**, the grass that is mowed after the first crop; **mead**, a place where grass is mowed; **meadow**, a small mead.

Met-an, to meet.—**Mote**, a meeting (an old word now found only in wardmote and folkmote); **meet**.

Reaf-ian, to take away.—**Reave**; **bereave**; **reef**, what is taken in in a sail; **rifle**, to plunder or take away; **robber**, a person who takes away what does not belong to him.

Sceot-an, to throw.—**Shoot**, to throw out (by means of a gun or otherwise); **shut**, to throw to (the door); **shoot**, a branch thrown out by a tree; shot, what is thrown out (by a gun or otherwise); shout, to throw out of the mouth; shuttle, an instrument thrown by a weaver; sheet, what is thrown over (a bed); shutter, what is thrown to, to guard a window.

Sit-an, to sit.—Sit; set, to make to sit; beset, to set about; onset, a setting on; overset, to turn over; upset; setter, a kind of dog; settle, a kind of seat; settle, to set or fix; settler; settlement; seat, the place where one sits.

Treow-an, believe.—Trow, to believe; true, what should be believed; truth; truthful; truthfully; truism; trust; intrust; trustee; trusty; trustworthy; troth.

Wac-an, to wake.—Wake; awake; awaken; wakeful; wakefulness; watch; watchful; watchfulness.

CHAPTER VI.

Prefixes and Suffixes.

PREFIXES.

1. ENGLISH (OR TEUTONIC).

A (a broken-down form of the A.S. preposition *on*), at, to, on, in, etc.; astern, abed, aboard, afield, afoot, ashore, alive, aweary.

After; afternoon, afterthought, aftermath, aftercrop.

At; atone (to bring together into one); ado (= at-do); twit (= at-wit).

Be, used both with nouns and with verbs—behalf, behoof, behest, bequest: betake, begin, become, bespatter, bedim, besprinkle, behead.

Down; downfall, downstroke, downcast.

For, not; forbid, forsake (not to seek), forget, forgo (wrongly spelled forego): or utterly: as, forlorn, fordone.

Fore, before; foretell, forefather, foresee, forebode, forecast, forenoon.

Gain, against; gainsay, gainstay (gainstand).

In, im, en, em; income, inlet, insight, inlay, inborn, inbred, into, ingraft, inlay, infold, imbed, endear, enthral, engrave, embower.

Mis, wrong; mislead, mistrust, misdeed, mishap, mistake.

Mid, in the middle of; midmost, midnight, midsummer, midday.

Off, from; offshoot, offset, offspring, offal (= off-fall), offhand.

Out; outset, outstrip, outvie, outrun, outdo.

Over; overwise, overfed, overmuch, overcoat, overhand, overseer, oversight.

Through, thorough; thoroughfare, throughout, thoroughbred, thoroughgoing.

To, this; to-day, to-night, to-morrow.

Un, (1) not; unclean, unwise, untrue, unbelief, unrest: or (2) back; undo, untie, unlock, unfold, unbind, unloose.

Under; undergrowth, underbred, underhand, undersell, underwood.

Up; uproar, upland, upstart, upset, upbear, upbraid, upright.

Wel, well; welfare, welcome, wellborn, well-bred, well-trained.

With, against; withstand, withdraw (drawing-room = withdrawing-room), withhold.

2. LATIN.

Ab (a, abs), from or away; averse, avert, aversion, abdicate, abstract, abstain, abjure, abate, abound. abuse, abduction.

Ad (ac, af, ag, al, am, an, ap, ar, as, at, a), to: adore, advise, accord, annex, accuse, accede, allude, allusion, announce, appear, assent, attend, aspire, affirm, affix, aggrieve, annul, ammunition, apparent, arrive, assume, assault, assumption, attend, attentive, attention, assimilate, attain, ascribe, avow.

Am (amb), round; ambient, amputate, ambition, ambiguous.

Ante (anti), before; antedate, antenuptial, antenatal, antechamber, antediluvian, anticipate.

Circum (circu), round; circumlocution, circumnavigate, circuit, circumvent, circuitous, circulate, circumference.

Con (col, com, cor, co), together with; consonant, connect, contend, conduct, compact, compound, commend, collision, collect, correct, corrupt, co-heir, coerce.

Contra (contro, counter), against; contradict, contravene, controversy, controvert, contraband, counterfeit.

De, down or from; denote, describe, depart, descent, devise, demure.

Dis (dif, di); disjoin, difficult, diffuse, divide, differ, dilute, dissent.

Ex (ef, e), out of; extort, exhume, efface, educe, extrude, extol, effect, education.

Extra, beyond; extraordinary, extravagant, extraneous.

In (il, im, ir, em, en), into; invade, incite, induce, illusion, illude, improve, impulse, impel, irruption, embrace, endure, encourage, embroil, irradiate, innate.

In (ig, il, im, ir), not; insecure, ignoble, illiterate, inconvenient, incurable, incapable, incapacitate, immortal, irregular, improper, illegitimate, irrational, innocent, infant.

Inter (intel, enter), between; intercourse, intelligent, interfere, interdict, enterprise, entertain, interrupt.

Intro, within; introduce.

Ob (oc, of, op, os), against; oblige, obtain, object, occur, offend, oppose, occult, offer, ostentation.

Pene, almost; as, peninsula.

Per (pel), through; perform, permit, pellucid, pertain.

Post, after; postpone, posthumous.

Præ or **pre**, before; prelection, preface, prevent, precede, premature, predict.

Præter or **preter**, beyond; preternatural, preterite.

Pro (por, pur, pol), forth, on or before; proceed, pollution, portend, purvey, portrait, purloin, purchase, pronoun, purpose.

Re (red), back; refute, result, redolent, redound, reduce, redeem.

Retro, backwards; retrograde, retrospect.

Se (sed), aside or apart; select, seclude, secede, seduce, sedition.

Sub (suc, suf, sug, sup, sur, sus, su), under, up from below; subject, suspect, succeed, suffer, suggest, suppose, suspend, suspect, succinct, suppress, surrogate, susceptible, subdue, suffuse, subtract, succour, supplant.

Subter, beneath; subterfuge.

Super (sur), over; superstructure, surplus, survive, superscribe, surfeit, surcharge, supernatural, surname, supercilious.

Trans (tra, tres); across; transmarine, translate, tradition, trespass, traduce.

Ultra, beyond; ultramontane, ultramarine.

Vice, instead of; viceroy, viceregal, viscount.

3. GREEK.

A or **an**, not; anarchy, anomaly, anonymous, apteryx (wingless), atheist.

Amphi, on both sides, round ; amphibious, amphitheatre.

Ana, up ; anatomy, analysis, anabasis, analyse.

Anti (ant), against ; antithesis, antipathy, . antarctic, antitype, antidote.

Apo (ap, aph), from ; apogee, apology, apostrophe, aphelion, aphorism.

Cata, down ; catarrh, catalepsy, catastrophe, catechism, cathartic, cathedral, catalogue.

Di (dis), two ; diphthong, dissyllable, dilemma, diploma.

Dia, through ; diameter, diagonal, diaphonous, diabolic, diagnosis, diastole, diaphragm.

En (el, em), in ; ellipse, emblem, energy, enthrone, empyrean, emphasis, emporium.

Endo, within ; endogenous.

Epi (ep), upon ; epilogue, epitaph, epiphany, epistle.

Exo, without ; exogenous, exotic.

Hyper, over or above ; hyperbola, hyperbole, hyperbolical, hypercritical, hyperborean.

Hypo (hyph), under ; hypotenuse, hypothesis, hypocrite, hyphen.

Meta (met, meth) signifies after, change ; metathesis, metonomy, method, metaphor.

Para (par), beside ; parabola, paraphrase, parhelion parody, parable.

Peri, round ; perimeter, peristyle, perigee, periphery, period.

Pro, before ; prologue, problem, prophet, program.

Pros, towards ; prosody, proselyte.

Syn (sy, syl, sym), together with ; syndic, syntax, symbol, syllogism, syllable, system, systole, synchronous, symptom, sympathy.

SUFFIXES.

4. ENGLISH (OR TEUTONIC).

Noun Suffixes.

1. Denoting a person or the doer of an action:

-er or **-ar** ; singer, baker, beggar, liar, lawyer, bowyer (a bow-maker), sawyer, sailor, speaker, miller, (fletcher = flechier, an arrow-maker).

-nd (old present participial ending); friend (= a loving person), fiend (= a hating person), errand, wind.

-ster (originally a *female* agent); Spinster, songster, maltster, huckster, baxter [= bakester], (now a term of contempt) ; youngster, gamester, punster.

-ter, **-ther**, **-der** ; daughter, father, spider (that is, spinder), mother, brother, foster (= foodster).

2. Denoting an instrument:

-der or **-er** ; ladder, rudder, bladder (from *blow*), feather, weather, rudder, murder, stair, finger (from *fangen*, to seize).

-el or **-le** ; shovel, girdle, shuttle, settle (a small seat), thimble.

3. Forming abstract nouns:

-dom ; kingdom, earldom, freedom, thraldom, wisdom, martyrdom, Christendom.

-hood, or **-head** ; manhood, boyhood, childhood, priesthood, Godhead, hardihood, neighbourhood, wifehood.

-ing ; hunting, blessing, standing, reading, clothing.

-ness ; witness (= a person who *wits*

or knows), wilderness, darkness, goodness, redness, weakness, hardness.

-red ; hatred, kindred.

-ship, -scape ; friendship, lordship, worship (= worthship), hardship, fellowship, landscape (in Milton, *landskip*: compare *skipper* for *shipper*).

-t, -th, -st, -d ; weight, height, sleight (from *sly*), gift, rift (from *rive*), theft, drought (from *dry*), frost, flight, warmth, health, width, death, birth, sloth (from *slow*), trust (from *trow*, to believe), flood (from *flow*), seed (from *sow*).

4. *Diminutives:*

-el or -le ; thimble (from *thumb*), riddle (from *read*).

-en ; maiden, kitten, chicken.

ing ; farthing, tithing (from *tithe* = tenth), riding (from *thrid* = third).

-kin ; lambkin, mannikin, pipkin.

-ling (= *l* + *ing*); darling (from *dear*), duckling, suckling, hireling, gosling, fatling, firstling, nestling, underling, starveling, suckling.

-ock ; bullock, hillock, paddock.

-y, -le ; lassie, Annie, Charlie, baby, Tommy, doggie.

Adjective Suffixes.

-d or -ed (originally a perfect participle-ending); hard, cold, loud : also added to nouns, as gifted, wretched, ragged, long-eared, feathered, landed.

-el or -le ; fickle, brittle, little, idle, mickle (from *much*).

-er ; lower, higher, brighter, sooner.

-er ; bitter, clever.

-ern, denoting the region of the globe : northern, eastern, southern, western.

-est ; lowest, highest, brightest, soonest.

-fold ; manifold, twofold, threefold, hundredfold, etc.

-ful ; scornful, sinful, wilful, truthful, tearful, needful, awful, dreadful, sorrowful.

-ish, -sh, or -ch, denotes partaking of the nature of; childish, foolish, slavish, swinish, churlish, waspish, whitish, goodish, brutish, girlish, boyish.

-less denotes destitute of; worthless, fearless, heedless, hopeless, tearless, sinless, godless, lawless, toothless.

-like, -ly, denotes like : warlike, childlike, womanly, manly, heavenly, godly, ghastly, likely.

-n or -en (also a perfect participle-ending); drunken, shaken, broken, molten, shorn, torn. It also denotes the material of which a thing is made, as golden, linen, wooden, silvern, flaxen, hempen, leathern.

-some denotes the possession of a quality ; wholesome, blithesome, gladsome, winsome, lissom (from *lithe*), buxom (that is, *buhsum*, from *bugan*, to bend), quarrelsome, tiresome.

-t (like d), probably perfect participial ending ; short (from *sceran*, to shear), blunt, tight, slight.

-ward denotes direction ; homeward, heavenward, seaward, northward, awkward (from *awk*, contrary), toward, froward (from *from*).

-y or -ey denotes the possession of a quality ; bloody, thirsty, guilty, woody, mighty, healthy, greedy, moody, sundry (from *sunder*), sticky, sorry (from *sore*), hairy, bushy, stony, clayey.

Verb Suffixes.

-el or -le gives a frequentative meaning to the verb ; waddle (from *wade*), startle, sparkle, dazzle (from *daze*), dribble (from *drip*), swaddle (from *swathe*), dapple (from *dip*), crawl, kneel (from *knee*), struggle, mingle, hurtle.

-en denotes making or doing ; fatten, broaden, soften, open (from *up*), lighten, sadden, gladden, sweeten, frighten, lengthen.

-er, also frequentative; glimmer, stagger, patter, flitter, flutter, wander, batter, sputter, stutter.

-k, also frequentative ; stalk (from *steal*), hark (from *hear*), walk.

Adverb Suffixes.

-ere denotes place in which ; here, there, where.

-es, -se, -ce, -s, which are old (possessive) genitive terminations ; sometimes, besides, unawares, else, twice (= twiẽs), thrice, hence, thence, whence, needs, outwards.

-ly denotes manner ; sweetly, sadly, cleanly.

-ther denotes direction towards : hither, thither, whither.

-ward, -wards, denote direction ; homeward, homewards, heavenward, heavenwards, hitherward, inwards.

-wise, -ways, denote manner or fashion ; otherwise, anywise, nowise, straightway, alway, always, sideways, lengthways.

5. LATIN.

Noun Suffixes.

1. *Those denoting persons or the doer of an action :*

-an, -ain; artisan, grammarian, villain.

-ant or -ent; agent, student, assistant, attendant, recreant, tenant, miscreant.

-ate, -ee, -ey, -y; legate, magistrate, advocate, curate, nominee, trustee, legatee, committee, attorney, covey, ally, deputy, jury.

-ess denotes a fem. agent ; governess, traitress, empress, duchess.

-ive, -iff; captive, fugitive, caitiff, plaintiff.

-tor, -sor, -or, -our, -er, -eer, -ier, -ar, -ary; doctor, successor, chancellor, emperor, actor, Saviour, founder, enchanter, governor, preacher, juror, author, monitor, victor, auditor, sponsor, engineer, auctioneer, grenadier, brigadier, registrar, usher, archer, farrier, vicar, premier, lapidary.

-trix, female agent ; executrix.

2. *Those forming Abstract Nouns :*

-age ; age, homage, savage, marriage, voyage, tillage, courage, personage, breakage, salvage. (Tonnage, bondage, shrinkage are hybrids.)

-ance, -ancy, -ence, -ency ; distance, constancy, infancy, consistence, resistance, decency, consistency, persistence, conveyance, cadence, chance (a form of cadence).

-ice, -ise ; avarice, service, merchandise, justice, exercise.

-ion, -tion, -sion, -som, -son, originally denoted the action of a verb; action, potion, opinion, poison, venison, malison, fusion, reason, tension, lection, ransom, season, position, nation, occasion.

-or, -our; labour, honour, ardour, savour, clamour, amour.

-tude ; servitude, latitude, fortitude, altitude, longitude, magnitude, custom (from *consuetudo*).

-ty, -ity; cruelty, charity, bounty, poverty, fealty, city, vanity.

-ure ; juncture, censure, culture, measure, cincture, picture, inclosure.

-y, -cy, -ce ; family, copy, memory, story, victory, misery, aristocracy, fancy, grace.

3. *Diminutives:*

-el, -le ; damsel, mongrel.

-et, -let ; pocket, rivulet.

-ette ; coquette, rosette.

-icle, -cule ; article, animalcule.

-ule ; globule, granule.

Adjective Suffixes.

-able, -ible, -ble; culpable, probable, flexible, edible, capable, soluble, feeble, amiable.

-acious denotes tendency, generally excessive; loquacious, veracious, vivacious, tenacious, voracious.

-al, -ar; comical, regal, legal, general, regular, singular, loyal, royal, equal, secular.

-an, -ane, -ain, -en, -on; human, urban, pagan, humane, mundane, certain, mizzen (from *medius*). Surgeon and sexton have become nouns.

-aneous, -ain -aign, -eign, -ange; cutaneous, mountain, champaign, foreign, strange.

-ant, -ent; volant, fluent, patent, innocent.

-ary, -arian, -arious; stationary, contrary, necessary, gregarious, agrarian.

-ate, -ete, -eet, -ite, -ute, -te; fortunate, deliberate, concrete, effete, discreet, erudite, minute, chaste.

-estrial, -estrian; terrestrial, equestrian.

-ic; civic, classic, barbaric, unique.

-id; fervid, morbid, acid, tepid.

-ile, -il, -eel, -le; servile, senile, fragile, civil, frail, genteel, gentle, able.

-ine denotes belonging to; feminine, divine, feline, lacustrine, canine, equine, saline.

-ive, inclined to; pensive, massive, captive, plaintive, restive, native, fugitive, active.

-ous, -ose, denote full of; famous, ingenuous, glorious, copious, assiduous, querulous, anxious, verbose, grandiose, jocose, dangerous.

-ory; illusory, amatory, admonitory.

-und; jocund, moribund, floribund, rotund.

Verb Suffixes.

-ate; advocate, complicate, anticipate, supplicate, eradicate.

-eer; domineer, career, volunteer.

-esce denotes the beginning of an action; effervesce, coalesce.

-fy denotes to make (from *facio*), magnify, terrify, qualify, signify.

-ish; nourish, perish, cherish, finish, flourish, banish, punish.

-ite, -ete, -t; expedite, delete, perfect, conduct, reflect, connect.

6. GREEK.

Noun Suffixes.

-et, -t, -ete, -ate, denote the agent; poet, prophet, athlete, comet, planet, apostate, æsthete (?), patriot.

-isk has diminutive signification; asterisk, obelisk.

-ism denotes the result of an action; deism, fatalism, egotism, criticism, aneurism.

-ist denotes the agent; baptist, sophist, evangelist.

-ma, -em, -me, -m, denote the result of an action; diorama, drama, dogma, system, scheme, theme, diadem, phlegm, enema.

-sis, -sy, -se, denote action; crisis, poesy, phase, genesis, emphasis, paralysis, hypocrisy, ellipse, phrensy.

-ter, -tre, denote the instrument; metre, centre.

Verb Suffixes.

-ise signifies to do; criticise, baptise, eulogise.

LITERATURE.

I.

Outline of Our Early Literature

(WITH ILLUSTRATIONS OF THE EARLY LANGUAGE).

1. THE BEOWULF.—The *Beowulf* is a poem which recounts the life and death of a hero of that name, who slays a monster called *Grendel*. It was a poetic legend brought from the Continent by our Teutonic ancestors. It does not seem to have been written down, or committed to paper, till the seventh century ; and it was probably preserved in the memory of different generations, by its being taught by fathers to their sons, and by the habit of chanting portions of it at the banquets of kings and warriors. It is a poem which in substance belongs to the Continental Teutons as much as to the English ; and it marks the point at which their literatures and languages begin to branch off. The scene is laid in the north of Denmark ; so that the poem is Northern, and not Southern, Teutonic. Its present form is due to a Christian writer of Northumbria. In literary form, therefore, it is English ; and is one of the earliest monuments of our literature. The poem consists of 6350 short lines, and is written throughout in head-rhymes,* or alliterative rhymes.

2. CÆDMON.—But the first true English poem was the work of a Northumbrian called CÆDMON, who was a servant to the monks of the abbey of Hilda, in Whitby. It was written about the year 670. It is a paraphrase of the history given in the Old and the New Testament. It sings of the creation of the world, of the history of Israel, of the life of Christ, of death, judgment, purgatory, heaven, and hell.

---

* In head-rhymes, two or three words in each line begin with the same letter.

3. **BÆDA.**—The oldest literature of a nation—the early writings of its childhood—are always poetic ; and prose-writings do not appear until the nation has, as it were, grown up. The first English prose-writer was BÆDA—or, as he is generally called, The Venerable Bede. He was born in the year 673. Like Cædmon, our first poet, he was a Northumbrian, and belonged to the monastery of Jarrow-upon-Tyne. His most important writings were in Latin ; and the best known of them is an *Ecclesiastical History of the English People.* But the work which makes Bæda our first writer of English prose, is a translation into English of the *Gospel of St John.* It was his last work ; and, in fact, he died just after he had dictated the last sentence. This was in the year 735.

4. **KING ALFRED.**—Up to the year 866, Northumbria was the home of learning and literature ; and the Northumbrian monks were its loving and diligent cultivators. But the incursions of the Danes, the destruction of the monasteries, and the perpetual danger to life and property arising from the troubled condition of the country, put a stop for some time to study and to letters. The cultivation of English as a book-language reappears, towards the end of the ninth century, in the south of the island. Alfred the Great, king of Wessex, is its great friend and promoter. Winchester was the capital of his kingdom ; and it was at Winchester that Alfred and his colleagues laboured at the writing of English books. He invited great scholars from different parts of the world ; he set up schools ; he himself taught a school in his own court ; he translated the Latin manuals of the time into English, and added largely to them from his own materials ; he translated also the *History* of the Venerable Bede ; and, most probably, he worked at the *Anglo-Saxon Chronicle,* and made it much fuller and more detailed than it had ever been before. He founded schools in the different parts of his kingdom, with the purpose and in the hope that 'every free-born youth, who has the means, may attend to his book till he can read English writing perfectly.' Alfred was born in the year 849, and died in 901. His own personal diligence—his unceasing head-work, are well known. He gave eight hours a

day to the work of public affairs—of managing the business
of his kingdom ; eight hours to books and study ; and he
reserved only eight hours for sleep, meals, exercise, and
amusement. The following is a passage from one of King
Alfred's writings :

Swa claenč heo waes othfeallen on Angel - cynne, thaet swithe feawa waeran be-heonan Humbre the hira thenunge cuthon understandan on Englisc, ohthe farthon an aerend-gewrit of Ledene on Englisc areccan ; and ic wene thaet naht monige be-geondan Humbre naeron.	So clean (completely) it was ruined (had ruin fallen) on the English folk (kin), that very few were on this side Humber who their service could understand in English, or out (forth) an epistle (errand-writing) from Latin into English declare (= translate) ; and I wene that not many beyond Humber were (who could do this).

5. **THE ANGLO-SAXON CHRONICLE.**—This chronicle was
written chiefly by monks, and was, in its earliest forms, a
dry register or record of events—of the births and deaths of
kings, bishops, earls, and other distinguished persons. In
Alfred's time, it became more of a history ; and even war-
songs and battle odes are quoted in it. It was continued
down to the death of King Stephen in 1154 ; and the last
portions of it were composed and transcribed by the monks
of Peterborough.

6. **ARCHBISHOP ÆLFRIC.**—Ælfric was Archbishop of Canterbury in the early part of the eleventh century ; and he translated the first seven books of the Bible, and part of Job,
into the oldest form of English, which is generally called
Anglo-Saxon. The following is a specimen :

1. On anginně gesceðp God heofenan and eordan.	In beginning shaped God heaven and earth.
4. God geseah thá, thaet hit gðd vaes, and he gedaeldě thaet leóht fram thám theóstrum.	God saw then, that it good was, and he dealed (divided) the light from the darkness.

7. **ANGLO-SAXON GOSPELS.**—This translation of the four
gospels forms another land-mark in the history of our
English tongue. This translation was made before the
Norman Conquest—before French words had come into our

language, and therefore before the inflections of English had dropped off from the words.

8. **OLD ENGLISH DIALECTS.**—For more than a century after the Conquest, English ceased to be used as a literary language—as a book-speech, except in the *Saxon Chronicle*, which was continued down to 1154. It still continued, of course, to be the language of the English nation. The Normans, when they used books at all, imported French books from France ; and they never dreamed that English was a language worthy to be written down. Different English counties spoke different kinds of English ; and this continued for many centuries—and still continues to a considerable extent. Thus the English spoken by a York-shire-man is very different from the English spoken by a Dorsetshire-man ; and the English of both differs very much from that spoken in Kent. But, in the eleventh and twelfth centuries—and even much later—travelling was very difficult and expensive ; working-men could not travel at all ; there was little motive to travel for any one ; and generations were born and died within the same village, or on one farm, or at least in one part of the ' country-side.' Thus different parts of this island pronounced their English in their own way ; had their own grammar—that is, their own inflections ; and each division of England looked upon itself as the right and correct speakers of the English tongue. But, among the large number of different dialects, there gradually emerged into distinct and even remarkable pro-minence three chief dialects. These are now known as the **Northern, Midland,** and **Southern.** The grammar of the three differs in several respects ; but the chief grammatical mark is found in the plural ending of the present tense of verbs. This is ës in the North ; en in the Midland dialect ; and eth in the South. Thus we have :

N.	*M.*	*S.*
We hopës,	we hopen,	we hopeth.
You hopës,	you hopen,	you hopeth.
They hopës,	they hopen,	they hopeth.

This variety of the plural forms the test which enables

readers of books written in the thirteenth and fourteenth
centuries, to determine in what part of England and in what
dialect they were written. The following are the chief books
written in these dialects :

NORTHERN (spoken between the Forth and the Humber)—
the Cursor Mundi, a version of Scripture in rhyme,
written about..1320

MIDLAND (spoken in the East-Anglian counties, and the
whole of the Midland district)—Orm's Ormulum, a
paraphrase in verse of the parts of the gospels given
in the church service, written in..................................1215

SOUTHERN (spoken in all the counties south of the Thames,
and also in several western counties)—Layamon's Brut
(a translation of a French poem by John de Wace),
written in..1205

9. THE FIRST ENGLISH BOOK AFTER THE NORMAN
CONQUEST.—Normandy was lost to England in the reign of
King John, in the year 1204. From that date, as we have
seen, there was a compulsion on the Norman-French to
forget their foreign origin, and to look upon themselves as
genuine Englishmen. A year after, in the year 1205, ten
years before the winning of the Magna Charta, appeared the
first work—it was a poem—that was written in English after
the Conquest. It is a translation by a Somersetshire priest
called Layamon or Laweman, from a French poem. *Brut* is
the French form of the name *Brutus*, who was said to be a
son of Æneas, and to be the founder of the British nation.
In those rude times, when history was quite unknown, the
origin of every nation was traced up to Troy, and the persons
of the *Iliad* of Homer. The *Brut* is a poem written chiefly
in head-rhymes, and consists of about thirty thousand lines.
But though it is translated from a French poem, there are
not fifty French words in the whole—that is, there is not
one French word in every six hundred lines.

10. ORM'S ORMULUM, 1215.—The *Ormulum* was a poem
written by an Augustine monk, called Orm or Ormin, and
called after his own name. It is a poem of nearly

twenty thousand short lines, without rhyme of any kind—
but with a regular number of accents. There are not five
French words in the whole poem. Orm was extremely
particular about his spelling; and, when an accent struck
a consonant after a *short* vowel, he insisted on doubling the
consonant.

11. LANGLAND AND CHAUCER.—William Langland represents the part of the nation that spoke pure English;
Geoffrey Chaucer, that part which spoke English with a large
admixture of Norman-French. In fact, Chaucer's poems
show the high-water mark of the French saturation of our
English vocabulary. Langland—a west-countryman, a monk,
a man of the people, and of intensely radical sympathies—was
born in 1332; Chaucer, a Londoner, in the very centre of
English society, page to the Duchess of Clarence at sixteen
years of age, and afterwards for great part of his life in court
employment, was born in 1340. Both died in the year 1400.
Langland's most important poem is the *Vision of (concerning)*
Piers Plowman. It is written in pure English, and in head-
rhyme. It is the last English poem that was written in
this kind of alliterative verse. The following lines are
taken from the introduction:

In a somer seasun	In a summer season
when softe was the sonně,	when soft was the sun,
I shop me into a schroud	I shape me into (dressed) shrouds (clothes)
a scheep as I werë,	shepherd as I was,
in habite of an hermite	in habit as a hermit,
unholy of werkes,	unholy in works,
wende I wydene in this world	went (far and) wide in this world,
wondrës to here.	wonders to hear.

Chaucer's great work is his *Canterbury Tales*, a series of
tales supposed to be told by a company of pilgrims to beguile
their journey to the shrine of St Thomas of Canterbury.
The company represented men and women of almost every
class in England; and their manners and character are
painted with wonderful truth and beauty. The following is
a passage from the *Prologue* to the *Canterbury Tales*; and

F

the French words are in italics. It is from the character of
the *Knight* :

> And evermore he had a *sovereyn prys*,[1]
> And, though that he was worthy, he was wys,
> And of his *port*[2] as meke as is a mayde.
> He nevere yit no *vileinye*[3] ne sayde
> In al his lyf, unto no *maner*[4] wight.
> He was a *verray perfight gentil*[5] knight.
> But, for to tellen you of his *array*,[6]
> His hors was good, but he ne was nought *gay*.[7]

12. ALLITERATION OR HEAD-RHYME.—Alliteration is the
correspondence of the first letter of several words in the same
line. It is like the well-known : ' Peter Piper picked a peck
of pepper off a pewter plate.'

> Round the rugged rocks the ragged rascals ran.

In Old English or Anglo-Saxon poetry it was the only kind
of rhyme used. The rhyme which is called end-rhyme was
not known to the Saxons, and was imported into England by
the Normans. In the ordinary Old English verse, the lines
are written in pairs, and in each pair there are usually three
alliterations, two in the first line and one in the second.
Even as late as the fourteenth century we find such verses
as the following, written by Langland :

> I shop me into a schroud,
> A scheep as I werë.

Shakspeare is fond of making fun of it. But it has
unconsciously survived in the language ; and there is not a
single great English poet, from Shakspeare to Tennyson, who
does not make a large use of it. Thus Shakspeare himself
has

> In maiden meditation, fancy-free.

> Full fathom five thy father lies.

and many other similar lines.

---

[1] The highest value. [2] Carriage. [3] Unbecoming or unkind thing.
[4] Kind of person. [5] Very perfect gentle. [6] Dress. [7] Gaily dressed.

Milton gives us such lines as :

> Him the Almighty power
> Hurled headlong flaming from the ethereal sky.

Shelley has the line :

> Our sweetest songs are those which tell of saddest thought.

Tennyson is very fond of alliteration. Thus, in the *Day-Dream :*

> And o'er them many a sliding star
> And many a merry wind was borne ; .
> And, streamed through many a golden bar,
> The twilight melted into morn.

13. JOHN GOWER.—A contemporary of Chaucer was John Gower, a gentleman of Kent. The date of his birth is not known ; but he survived Chaucer eight years, dying in 1408. He wrote the *Lover's Confession* in English verse ; the *Mirror of the Meditative Man* in French verse (lost) ; the *Voice of one crying*, in Latin. His style was heavy and prosaic. Chaucer called him the 'moral Gower.'

14. JOHN BARBOUR.—Another eminent contemporary of Chaucer was John Barbour, Archdeacon of Aberdeen, who wrote in the Scottish, or Northern English, form of our tongue. He was a learned man, and a man of the world, who filled important office in the employment of the Scottish king. His great work was a narrative poem, *The Bruce*, giving an account of the life and adventures of the great Bruce. It is valuable both as a monument of our language and a storehouse of historical incident. Barbour died about 1395. The literature of Scotland was worthily continued by the royal poet, James I. (1394–1437), brought up as a prisoner in England, and well educated. His great work was the *King's Quhair* (or book), a poem in the style and in one of the metres of Chaucer.

15. SIR JOHN MANDEVILLE.—Sir John Mandeville is the first writer of the *new* English prose—the prose with a large addition of French words. He is sometimes called the Father of English Prose. He was born at St Albans, in Hertfordshire, in 1300, and died at Liège, in 1372. He was a great

traveller, soldier, and physician; travelled through the Holy
Land, served under the Sultan of Egypt and the Great Khan
of Cathay (the old name for *China*); and wandered through
almost all the then known parts of Europe, Asia, and Africa.
He wrote his travels in three languages—first in Latin for
the learned; then in French for the Norman-French; and
lastly in English, 'that every man of the nation might
understand them.' The following is a specimen of his prose:

And 2 myle from Ebron (Hebron) is the grave of Lothe (Lot) that
was Abrahames brother. And a lytille fro Ebron is the mount of
Mambre, of the whiche the valeye takethe his name. And there is a
tree of oke, that the Sarazinis clepen (call) *Dirpê*, that is of Abrahames
tyme, the whiche men clepen the drye tree. And thei saye, that it
hathe ben there sithe the beginnynge of the world, and was sumtyme
grene, and bare leves, unto the tyme that oure Lord dyede on the
cros; and thanne it dryede, and so dyden alle the trees, that weren
thanne in the world.

This is almost quite like modern English—with the exception of the spelling.

16. JOHN WICLIFFE.—John Wicliffe,* or John de Wycliffe,
was born at the village of Hipswell, near Richmond, in Yorkshire, in the year 1324. He died at the vicarage of Lutterworth,
in Leicestershire, in the year 1384, at the age of sixty. He
was the first Englishman who attempted to make a complete
translation of the Scriptures. Of this work, however, the
Gospels alone can be certainly identified as the work of
Wicliffe himself. The Old Testament and apocryphal books
were translated principally by Nicolas de Hereford, and it
is supposed that his work was interrupted in 1382, and
that the Bible was completed about that time by extracting
the text of the gospels from Wicliffe's commentary on the
gospels (written in 1360), and adding to it a new translation of the rest of the New Testament. A later version
was finished by Wicliffe's friend, John Purvey, about 1388,
and appears to be mainly a revision of the work of Hereford
and Wicliffe. The later is a less close and literal version
than the former, and is expressed in more idiomatic and
less laboured English.

17. OUR ENGLISH BIBLE AND ITS HISTORY.—The first fresh translation from the original sources was that of William Tyndale. His New Testament, printed at Cologne and at Worms, reached the English shores in 1526, and was followed three years later by the Pentateuch. To this translation our authorised version owes much of its peculiar force and beauty. The first complete English Bible was that of Miles Coverdale, which appeared in 1535. In April 1539 appeared the Great Bible (so called from its large size), prepared by Coverdale at Paris, but completed in London under the patronage of Thomas Cromwell. The translation of the psalms in the Great Bible has remained, without alteration, the Psalter in the Book of Common Prayer. During the last year of Mary's reign and the beginning of Elizabeth's, the English refugees at Geneva completed a fresh revision of the Great Bible, which was published in 1560, in a handy size, with a marginal commentary, and the chapters divided into verses. The Genevan version (sometimes called the Breeches Bible), became popular with the Puritans, and more than two hundred editions of it were published, and it gave way slowly before the present authorised version. Soon after Elizabeth's accession, Archbishop Parker organised a revision of the Great Bible of 1539, which was published in 1568, and became known as the Bishops' Bible. During Elizabeth's reign, the Popish exiles at Rheims produced a new version from the Vulgate, which was printed at Douay in 1609, and is known as the Douay Bible. The English Bible which is now recognised as the 'authorised version' wherever the English language is spoken, is a revision of the Bishops' Bible, begun in 1604 and finished in 1611. Of this noble version many millions have been printed, and its general acceptance by all English-speaking people is the best testimony to its excellence. No book has had so great an influence on our language and literature; its words and phrases have been preserved in our vocabulary, and are the most familiar to our ears, consecrated as they are with the associations of two hundred and seventy years. A revision of our version by the most eminent scholars is now in progress, and the revised

New Testament was published, May 17, 1881. Appended is
a passage from Romans (xii. 6—8), as it appears in Wicliffe's,
Tyndale's, the Great Bible, the Genevan Bible, the Bishop's
Bible, and our Authorised Version :

1. WICLIFFE.

6 **Therfor** we that han yiftis dyuer-
synge, aftir the grace that is youun to
vs, **ethir** prophecie, aftir the resoun of
feith ;

7 ethir seruise, in mynystryng ;
ethir he that techith, in techyng ;

8 he that stirith softli, in mone-
styng ; he that yyueth, in symplenesse ;
he that is souereyn, in bisynesse ; he
that hath merci, in gladnesse.

2. TYNDALE.

6 Seyinge that we have divers
gyftes accordynge to the grace that
is geven vnto vs, yf eny man have
the gyft off prophesy lett hym have it
that itt be agreynge vnto the fayth.

7 **Let hym that** hath an office,
wayte on his office. Let hym that
teacheth take hede to his doctryne.

8 **Let hym that** exhorteth geve
attendaunce to his exhortacion. Yf
eny man geve, lett hym do it with
singlenes. Let hym that rueleth do
it with diligence. Yf eny man shewe
mercy lett hym do itt with cherfulnes.

3. GREAT BIBLE.

6 Seynge that we haue dyuers gyftes
accordynge to the grace that is geuen
vnto vs : yf any man haue the gyfte of
prophecy let him haue it that it be
agreing vnto ye fayth.

7 Let hym that hath an office wayte
on hys office. Let hym that teacheth
take hede to hys doctrine.

8 Let hym that exhorteth geue
attendaunce to his exhortacion. If
any man geue, let hym do it wyth
synglenes. Let hym that ruleth do it
with diligence. If any man shewe
mercy, let him do it with cherfulnes.

4. GENEVAN BIBLE.

6 Seeing then that we haue giftes
that are diuers, according to the grace
that is giuen vnto vs whether we haue
prophesie, let us prophesie according
to the proportion of faith :

7 Or an office let vs waite on the
office : or hee that teacheth on teaching.

8 Or he that exhorteth on exhorta-
tion : hee that distributeth let him do
it with simplicitie : he that ruleth with
diligence : hee that sheweth mercie
with chearefulnes.

5. BISHOPS' BIBLE.

6 Seeing that wee haue diuers giftes
according to the grace that is giuen
vnto vs eyther prophecie, after the
measure of fayth,

7 Eyther office, in administration :
or he that teacheth, in teaching.

8 Or he that exhorteth, in exhorting :
he that giueth in singlenesse, he that
ruleth in diligence : hee that is mercy-
full in chearefulnesse.

6. AUTHORISED VERSION.

6 Hauing then gifts differing according to the grace that is giuen to vs,
whether prophecie, let vs prophecie
according to the proportion of faith.

7 Or ministery, let vs wait, on our
ministring : or hee that teacheth on
teaching.

8 Or he that exhorteth, on exhorta-
tion : he that giueth let him doe it
with simplicite ; hee that ruleth, with
diligence : hee that sheweth mercy
with cheerefulnesse.

I I.

Tabular Outline of Modern English Literature.

(Poems are mentioned in *Italics*.)

WILLIAM DUNBAR,
Poet.   **1450—1530.**

The Thistle and the Rose (1503); *The Golden Terge* (1508); *The Dance of the Seven Deadly Sins.* The greatest of the Scottish poets except Burns. He has been called 'the Chaucer of Scotland.'

SIR THOMAS MORE,
Barrister; Lord   **1480—1535.**
Chancellor of England; writer on social philosophy; historian.

History of King Edward V., and of his brother, and of Richard III. (1513); Utopia (1516)—a description of a model state of society, written to influence the bettering of the laws of England.

WILLIAM TYNDALE,
Priest; translator;   **1477—1536.**
author.

Translation of New Testament (1525, 1534), also of the Pentateuch and Jonah (1530–31). He has done more by his version to fix and shape our language in its present form, than any writer between Chaucer and Shakspeare.

SIR DAVID LYNDSAY,
Keeper of Prince   **1490—1556.**
James (afterwards James V. of Scotland); Lyon king-at-arms; poet.

Satire of the Three Estates, that is, King, Lords, and Commons; *Monarchie.*

ROGER ASCHAM,
Lecturer   on   **1515—1568.**
Greek at Cambridge; tutor to Edward VI. and Queen Elizabeth.

Toxophilus, a treatise on shooting with the bow; The Schoolmaster, a book about teaching, especially the teaching of Latin.

| JOHN FOX, **1517—1587.** | Book of Martyrs (1563), an account of the chief Protestant martyrs, chiefly those in the reign of Mary. |

JOHN FOX, 1517—1587.
Prebendary of Salisbury Cathedral.

Book of Martyrs (1563), an account of the chief Protestant martyrs, chiefly those in the reign of Mary.

EDMUND SPENSER, 1552—1599.
Secretary to Viceroy of Ireland; poet.

Shepherd's Calendar (1579); *Faerie Queene* (1590–96), in six books.

RICHARD HOOKER, 1553—1600.
Scholar and theologian; Master of the Temple; and rector of a country church.

Laws of Ecclesiastical Polity. This is a defence of the Church of England, and contains passages of great majesty and splendour of diction.

SIR PHILIP SIDNEY, 1554—1586.
Courtier; romancist; poet.

Arcadia, a romance (1580); Defence of Poesie. Some *Sonnets*.

FRANCIS BACON, 1561—1626.
Lord High Chancellor of England; essayist; philosopher.

Essays (1597); Advancement of Learning (1605); Novum Organum (1620); and other works on philosophy, and the art of gaining new knowledge.

SIR WALTER RALEIGH, 1552—1618.
Courtier; navigator; historian.

History of the World (1614), written in the Tower of London, where he lay for about thirteen years. His work is 'one of the finest models of our quaint and stately old English style.'

WILLIAM SHAKSPEARE, 1564—1616.
Dramatist and poet; born at Stratford-on-Avon; went to London at the age of twenty-two; left London in 1609, and from that time lived in his native town.

Tragedies and *Comedies*, and *Historical Plays;* thirty-seven in all. Among his greatest tragedies are, *Hamlet, Lear, Macbeth, Othello, Romeo and Juliet.* Of his comedies the best are the *Tempest, Midsummer Night's Dream, As you like it, Merchant of Venice,* &c. Of his historical plays, *Richard III.* and *Julius Cæsar* are specially worth mention. *Minor Poems.* Wrote no prose.

BEN JONSON, 1574—1637.
Dramatist ; poet ;
prose-writer.

Tragedies and Comedies, of the latter, the greatest are *Volpone or the Fox; Every Man in His Humour;* and *The Alchemist.*

WILLIAM DRUMMOND,
Poet. **1585—1649.**

Sonnets and *Religious Poems.*

SIR THOMAS BROWNE,
Medical practi- **1605—1682.**
tioner at Norwich.

Religio Medici (the religion of a physician), contains the author's opinions on a great variety of subjects ; Urn Burial, a learned and eloquent work.

JOHN MILTON, 1608—1674.
Poet ; Latin
secretary to
Cromwell (1649).
Became blind in
1654.

Minor Poems; Paradise Lost; Paradise Regained; Samson Agonistes. Many prose works, chiefly on politics, and in defence of the Commonwealth.

THOMAS HOBBES,
Philosopher. **1588—1679.**

Leviathan (1651), a great philosophical and political work.

JEREMY TAYLOR,
Bishop of Down **1613—1667.**
in Ireland.

Holy Living and Holy Dying (1649); and many other books and sermons.

SAMUEL BUTLER,
Secretary to the **1612—1680.**
Earl of Carberry.

Hudibras (1663), a mock-heroic poem, written to caricature the Puritans.

JOHN DRYDEN, 1631—1700.
Poet - laureate
and Historio-
grapher Royal.
Also a play-
wright ; poet ;
prose-writer;
critic.

Annus Mirabilis (1667)—a poem on the *Plague* and the *Fire of London; Absalom and Achitophel* (1681)—a poem on political matters; *Hind and Panther* (1687). He wrote many *Tragedies* and *Comedies* and *Odes;* a translation of the *Æneid* of Virgil. He wrote a great deal of the best prose—chiefly Essays and Introductions to his poems.

JOHN BUNYAN,
Tinker and **1628—1688.**
preacher.

The Pilgrim's Progress (1678); the Holy War, and other works.

JOHN LOCKE, 1632–1704.
Member of the Board of Trade; one of the leading men in English philosophy.

Letters on Toleration (1689); Essay concerning the Human Understanding (1690); Thoughts concerning Education, and other prose works.

DANIEL DEFOE, 1661–1731.
Pamphleteer; journalist; had a very troubled and changeful career.

Robinson Crusoe (1719); *The True-born Englishman*; Journal of the Plague; The Shortest Way with the Dissenters; and more than a hundred books and pamphlets in all. He is one of the most taking writers that ever lived.

JONATHAN SWIFT, 1667–1745.
Dean of St Patrick's in Dublin; satirist; poet; prose-writer.

Battle of the Books; Tale of a Tub (1704); Gulliver's Travels (1726). Many of the ablest political pamphlets of the day. A number of *Poems*. His prose was the strongest and most nervous prose written in the eighteenth century.

SIR RICHARD STEELE, 1671–1729.
Gentleman usher to Prince George; a fashionable man about town.

Essays in the Tatler, in the Spectator, in the Guardian—all of them a kind of magazine. A few plays.

JOSEPH ADDISON, 1672–1719.
Secretary of State.

Essays in the Tatler, in the Spectator, and in the Guardian. *Cato*: a tragedy (1713). Several short *Poems*. His prose is the finest, most genial, and most delicate of all the prose-writings of the eighteenth century.

ALEXANDER POPE, 1688–1744.
Poet; a Roman Catholic.

Essay on Criticism (1711); *Rape of the Lock*—the story of the stealing of a lock of hair; *Translations of the Iliad and Odyssey*, half of the latter done by assistants (1715–20); the *Dunciad*; *Essay on Man*. A few essays in prose; and a volume of Letters.

JAMES THOMSON, 1700—1748.
Poet; held sinecure offices under government.

The Seasons—a poem in blank verse; *The Castle of Indolence*, a poem in the nine-lined stanza of Edmund Spenser.

HENRY FIELDING, 1707—1754.
Novelist and journalist.

Many comedies—now forgotten. Joseph Andrews (1742); Tom Jones (1749); Amelia (1751). He was the 'first great English novelist, and he remains to this day one of the greatest.'

DAVID HUME, 1711—1776.
Librarian; secretary to the British Embassy in France.

Treatise of Human Nature (1737); Essays (1742); Inquiry concerning the Principles of Morals; History of England (1754-62). Writes very clear and pleasant prose.

DR SAMUEL JOHNSON, 1709—1784.
Schoolmaster; literary man; dictionary-maker.

London (1738); the *Vanity of Human Wishes;* The Rambler (1750-52); The Idler; English Dictionary (1755); Rasselas, a kind of novel; Lives of the Poets; and other prose works.

THOMAS GRAY, 1716—1771.
Poet; letter-writer; professor of Modern History, Cambridge.

Odes; Elegy written in a Country Churchyard, one of the most pleasing, perfect, and oft-quoted poems in the language. He was also a good letter-writer.

WILLIAM ROBERTSON, 1721—1793.
Clergyman; historian; Principal of the University of Edinburgh.

History of Scotland (1759); History of Charles V. (1769); History of America (1777). Most readable and fluent prose.

TOBIAS GEORGE SMOLLETT, 1721—1771.
Medical practitioner; poet; pamphleteer; critic and novelist.

Roderick Random; Peregrine Pickle; and Humphrey Clinker. His novels are notable for their broad humour, and an easy picturesque style of narration.

ADAM SMITH, 1723—1790.
Professor of Logic in the University of Glasgow; then of Moral Philosophy.

Theory of Moral Sentiments (1759); Enquiry into the Nature and Causes of the Wealth of Nations (1776). The founder of the science of economics (or wealth of nations).

OLIVER GOLDSMITH,
Poet ; literary **1728—1774.**
man ; play-writer.

The Vicar of Wakefield (1766); the *Deserted Village;* She Stoops to Conquer, a comedy. The *Traveller;* Citizen of the World; Histories and minor *Poems.* The writer of the most pleasant prose of the eighteenth century.

EDMUND BURKE,
Statesman; 'the **1730—1797.**
first man in the
C o m m o n s ;'
writer on poli-
tical philosophy.

Essay on the Sublime and Beau-tiful (1756); Reflections on the French Revolution (1790). Many speeches, pamphlets, and articles on political matters. One of the deepest political thinkers, most eloquent speakers, and ornate writers of prose that ever lived.

WILLIAM COWPER,
Poet. **1731—1800.**

Truth, the *Progress of Error* (1781), and other poems; the *Task* (1785); *John Gilpin; Translations of the Iliad and Odyssey* (1791) in blank verse ; *Hymns.* His prose — which consists of letters—is clear, humorous, and pleasant.

EDWARD GIBBON,
Historian; sat **1737—1794.**
eight years in the
House of Com-
mons, but never
spoke.

Decline and Fall of the Roman Empire (1776–87); Essays on the Study of Literature (in French). His style is a splen-did example 'of smiting phrases and weighty antithesis.'

ROBERT BURNS,
Ploughman; **1759—1796.**
farmer; Excise
officer; poet.

Poems and *Songs* (1786–96) (*Cottar's Saturday Night, Jolly Beggars, Tam o' Shanter, Mountain Daisy,* etc.) His prose consists chiefly of letters.

WILLIAM WORDSWORTH,
Distributor of **1770—1850.**
stamps for the
county of West-
moreland; poet;
poet-laureate.

Descriptive Sketches (1793) ; *Lyri-cal Ballads* (1798); *Sonnets; The Excursion* (1814); *The Prelude.* He marks the dawn of a new school of poetry in the nineteenth century.

SAMUEL TAYLOR COLERIDGE
Journalist; secretary; literary man; poet. **1772—1834.**

The Ancient Mariner and *Christabel* (1797—1806); several plays, including a translation of Schiller's *Wallenstein;* many minor poems; The Friend—a set of essays; Confessions of an Inquiring Spirit; Biographia Literaria; Aids to Reflection. His prose is very elaborate and also very musical.

ROBERT SOUTHEY,
Literary man; historian; reviewer; poet; poet-laureate. **1774—1843.**

Joan of Arc (1793); *Thalaba the Destroyer;* the *Curse of Kehama;* Life of Nelson. Firm, clear, and sensible prose. Wrote more than a hundred volumes.

CHARLES LAMB,
Clerk in the East India House; essayist and humorist. **1775—1835.**

Essays of Elia (1820-25), which are quaint and familiar, and full of kindly wit and grotesque humour.

SIR WALTER SCOTT,
Advocate; poet; novelist. **1771—1832.**

Border Minstrelsy—a collection of old Border ballads (1802); *Lay of the Last Minstrel* (1805); *Marmion* (1808); the *Lady of the Lake* (1810); Waverley (1814)—the first of that remarkable series, the Waverley Novels. In verse, he is the 'Homer of Scotland;' and he was a master of most fluent, bright, flowing narrative prose.

THOMAS CAMPBELL,
Poet; literary man. **1777—1844.**

Pleasures of Hope (1799); *Minor Poems*—such as *Hohenlinden, Battle of the Baltic, Ye Mariners of England, Gertrude of Wyoming* (1809). His prose consists chiefly of the Introductions to his *Specimens of the British Poets.*

THOMAS MOORE,
Poet; biographer; historian. **1779—1852.**

Odes and Epistles (1806); *Lalla Rookh* (1817); Life of Byron (1830); *Irish Melodies* (1834); History of Ireland (1836).

LORD BYRON, 1788–1824.
(George Gordon).
Peer ; poet.

English Bards and Scotch Reviewers (1808); *Childe Harold* (1812); the *Bride of Abydos* (1814); and many *Plays.* His prose—which is full of vigour, fire, and eloquence — consists chiefly of letters.

PERCY BYSSHE SHELLEY,
Poet. 1792–1822.

Queen Mab (1813); *Revolt of Islam*; *Prometheus Unbound* (1819)—a tragedy; *Odes (The Cloud, To the Skylark,* etc.), and many minor poems. His prose consists chiefly of letters.

HENRY HALLAM,
Historian ; liter- 1778–1859.
ary man ; Trustee
of the British
Museum.

View of the State of Europe during the Middle Ages (1818) ; Constitutional History of England (1827) ; Literature of Europe (1837) ; History of the Middle Ages (1848). A clear and impartial writer.

THOMAS DE QUINCEY,
Literary man. 1785–1859.

Confessions of an English Opium-eater (1821) ; Essays on subjects in almost every department of History, Philosophy, and Literature. His style is eloquent, musical, and elaborate. In his own way, he was the finest prose-writer of the nineteenth century.

JOHN KEATS, 1795–1821.
Poet.

Endymion (1818); *Hyperion; Eve of St Agnes; Odes.* His poems are full of beauty and rich and picturesque imagery.

THOMAS CARLYLE,
Mathematician ; 1795–1881.
literary man ; re-
viewer; historian.

Sartor Resartus (1833) ; The French Revolution, a History (1837) ; Oliver Cromwell's Letters and Speeches (1845) ; Life of John Sterling (1851) ; History of Friedrich II. of Prussia (1858–65). His style is full of force, fire, and grotesqueness ; he paints in vivid colours, and presents a true and exact picture of the living man.

LORD MACAULAY, 1800–1859.
Barrister; reviewer; Secretary of the Board of Control for India; member of the Supreme Council of India; historian; peer.

Essay on Milton (1825); *Lays of Ancient Rome* (1842); Essays (1843); History of England (1848-1859). Wrote a style of the greatest force and picturesqueness—full of allusion, illustration, grace, clearness, and point.

LORD LYTTON, 1805–1873.
Novelist; poet; statesman.

Eugene Aram (1831); The Last Days of Pompeii; The Caxtons; some plays, minor *Poems*, and essays. Writes a most clear, fluent, bright, ornate, and readable English style.

JOHN STUART MILL, 1806–1873.
Clerk in the East India House; Utilitarian philosopher.

System of Logic (1843); Political Economy (1844); Essay on Liberty. One of the foremost thinkers of his time.

HENRY WADSWORTH LONGFELLOW, 1807–1882.
Professor of Modern Languages and Literature; poet.

Evangeline (1847); *Hiawatha* (1855); *Minor Poems (Excelsior; A Psalm of Life, etc.)* One of the sweetest and best known of American poets.

ALFRED TENNYSON, 1809–
Poet; poet-laureate.

Poems, chiefly Lyrical (1830); *In Memoriam* (1850); *Idylls of the King* (1859-73); *Enoch Arden* (1864); and several dramas. His poetical style is full of beauty, sweetness, and variety.

ELIZABETH BARRETT BROWNING, 1809–1861.
Poetess; the wife of Robert Browning.

Poems (1838); *Aurora Leigh* (1856); *The Cry of the Children; Cowper's Grave; Sonnets from the Portuguese*, etc. A poetess of infinite sweetness and power.

ROBERT BROWNING, 1812–
Poet.

Pauline (1833); *Paracelsus* (1836); *The Ring and the Book*, and about two dozen more volumes. His poems are very difficult to understand, but are very well worth understanding.

WILLIAM MAKEPEACE THACKERAY, 1811–1863. Novelist.	Vanity Fair (1846); Pendennis (1849); Esmond; English Humorists, etc. The finest novelist and one of the best prose-writers of the century.
CHARLES DICKENS, Novelist. 1812–1870.	Pickwick Papers (1837); Oliver Twist; Nicholas Nickleby; David Copperfield; Dombey and Son; Christmas Books, etc. He has been read over and over again by hundreds of thousands of delighted readers.
JOHN RUSKIN, 1819– Art-critic; moralist; literary man.	Modern Painters (1843); The Seven Lamps of Architecture; The Stones of Venice (1851–53); Sesame and Lilies; Lectures on Art; Fors Clavigera. One of the most wonderful and imaginative writers of English prose that ever lived.
GEORGE ELIOT (Marian Evans), 1820–1880. Novelist.	Adam Bede (1858); Middlemarch (1871); Daniel Deronda (1876); *Poems.* The novels of this accomplished lady rank among the greatest of modern times.

THE END.

Edinburgh
Printed by W & R. Chambers.

www.ingramcontent.com/pod-product-compliance
Lightning Source LLC
Chambersburg PA
CBHW032240080426
42735CB00008B/932